C000220134

# LOST RA
# OF
# MERSEYSIDE
# AND GREATER
# MANCHESTER

Gordon Suggitt

COUNTRYSIDE BOOKS
NEWBURY, BERKSHIRE

COUNTRYSIDE BOOKS
3 Catherine Road
Newbury, Berkshire


To view our complete range of books,
please visit us at
www.countrysidebooks.co.uk


ISBN 1 85306 869 1

The cover picture shows Black Five no 44717 heading through
Stockport Tiviot Dale in the early 1950s
(From an original painting by Colin Doggett)

Designed by Mon Mohan
Maps by the author

Produced through MRM Associates Ltd., Reading
Typeset by Techniset Typesetters, Newton-le-Willows
Printed by Woolnough Bookbinding Ltd., Irthlingborough

# CONTENTS

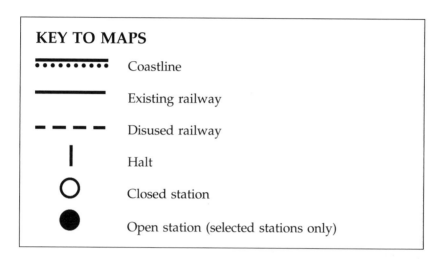

**KEY TO MAPS**

Coastline

Existing railway

Disused railway

Halt

Closed station

Open station (selected stations only)

# ACKNOWLEDGEMENTS

I would like to acknowledge the help and resources provided by the libraries of Merseyside and Greater Manchester. I would also like to thank individually John Ward for the use of his photo collection and reminiscences, Neil Cain for his help with his Uncle Stanley Morris's recollections, Ron Hunt for the use of his photo collection, Mrs Shirley Peden and Paul Shackcloth for their help with photo copyright and Mike Clark for help with loco identification. Lastly I am again especially grateful to my wife Jen for her continued help, encouragement and careful checking of the text.

# ABBREVIATIONS

The following abbreviations are used in this book:

| | |
|---|---|
| BR | British Railways |
| CLC | Cheshire Lines Committee |
| ELR | East Lancashire Railway |
| GCR | Great Central Railway |
| GNR | Great Northern Railway |
| GWR | Great Western Railway |
| HMRS | Historical Model Railway Society |
| L&M | Liverpool & Manchester Railway |
| LMS | London, Midland & Scottish Railway |
| LNER | London & North Eastern Railway |
| LNWR | London & North Western Railway |
| LOR | Liverpool Overhead Railway |
| LUR | Lancashire Union Railway |
| LYR | Lancashire & Yorkshire Railway |
| MD&HB | Mersey Docks & Harbour Board |
| MLR | Manchester & Leeds Railway |
| MS&L | Manchester, Sheffield & Lincolnshire Railway |
| MSDR | Manchester South District Railway |
| OA&GB | Oldham, Ashton & Guide Bridge Junction Railway |
| ST&AJ | Stockport, Timperley & Altrincham Junction Railway |
| WJR | Wigan Junction Railway |

# Introduction

The cradle of Britain's railways? Not 'birthplace', as this would perhaps be North East England, where the Stockton & Darlington Railway opened as the country's first steam-hauled public railway in 1825. Instead the term 'cradle' would refer to the ten years after that, often thought of as a period of transition before the development of a national network. During that time, the area covered by this book saw the construction of six separate lines, most notably the Liverpool & Manchester Railway of 1830. Most regions of the country experienced only one or two such developments, the Canterbury & Whitstable Railway in South East England for example, while London did not have a single railway. Yet within the next six years, the capital was linked by rail to Brighton, Southampton, Bristol, Birmingham, Preston, Leeds and York. These lines were using innovations pioneered on the North West's early railways, for example the 'six-foot' space between running lines introduced on the Wigan Branch Railway of 1832.

The route of the Wigan Branch Railway still exists as part of the West Coast Main Line. The former Liverpool & Manchester Railway is also a working line, but many of its 'firsts' were connected with Manchester's Liverpool Road station, which is included here as a closed terminus. Others of the original six lines did close and are featured in the pages that follow – the Bolton & Leigh Railway (1828), the Leigh & Kenyon Junction Railway (1831) and the St Helens Railway (1833). Not all the lines covered here are that historic; for example the Midland line through Cheadle Heath did not open until the 20th century.

The places mentioned above give some indication of the geographical scope of this book. The 'Merseyside' and 'Greater Manchester' refer to regions as defined by the two counties of those names set up in 1974. These no longer exist but their areas are still in everyday use by police and fire brigade authorities, plus transport organisations and local radio stations, and have been broadly used for this book. However, closed railway lines do not conform to county boundaries, especially ones drawn well over a century after most of them were built, and some adjustment has been necessary. The previously published 'Lancashire' volume in this series included Horwich, Holcombe Brook, Ramsbottom and most notably Southport, which are not repeated here. Instead this book extends into present-day Cheshire to cover destinations at Hooton, Widnes and Glazebrook.

This is of course a largely urban and industrial area. Rural railways were few and far between, with instead a multitude of mineral and freight lines serving mills, works, mines and docks. These in general have been omitted, with the emphasis confined to those closed lines that at some time had a regular passenger service. (The mineral lines of the coalfield areas have been comprehensively covered elsewhere – see Bibliography.) This book covers some forty closed railways, ranging from single-track branches to former main lines. The order in which they are dealt with is roughly arranged west to east, starting by the Dee estuary and finishing only a couple of miles from the Derbyshire boundary. Many stretches of old railway can be walked, and 'sights' include preserved stations (both large and small), tunnels and viaducts, but very little in the way of preserved railways. Only the East Lancashire Railway and its Heywood extension currently represent the preservation scene, so this book is largely concerned with non-operating reminders of the railway past, starting in Merseyside's rural fringes.

Gordon Suggitt

# 1
# On The Wirral

*Hooton to West Kirby*
*Birkenhead Woodside*
*The Seacombe branch*

*The railways' entry point for the Wirral – Hooton station around 1930, with a West Kirby platform at the left, and one of four used by Birkenhead Woodside trains to the right. (Stations UK)*

## Hooton to West Kirby

The Wirral is the peninsula between the Mersey and Dee estuaries, and is currently partly in Merseyside's Metropolitan Borough of Wirral, with the rest in Cheshire. Its western half is still largely rural, and the railway through it was regarded as one of the region's few country branch lines. The eastern terminus,

9

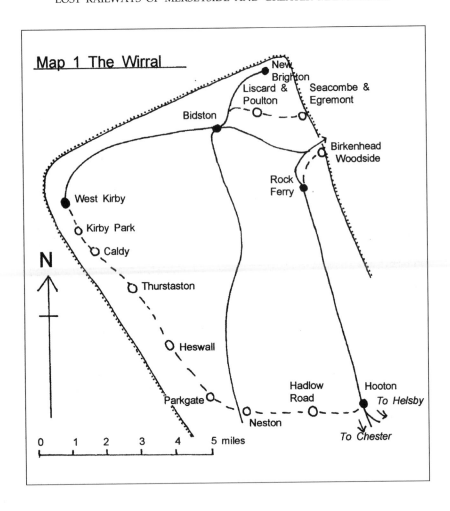

Map 1 The Wirral

Hooton, began as a station on the Chester & Birkenhead line of 1840, which in 1860 became the GWR/LNWR Birkenhead Joint line. The two companies obtained an Act in 1862 for a 4½ mile single-track branch from Hooton to Parkgate, which had been a minor port for the nearby Wirral colliery. When the Dee estuary silted up in the 1840s, an alternative outlet was required. The branch was opened in 1866, with intermediate stations at Hadlow Road and Neston, and a line almost a mile south to

10

*The Great Western on the Wirral – 'Metropolitan' 2-4-0T no 1401 on a local service at Thurstaston early in the 20th century. (J. Ryan collection)*

the colliery. Meanwhile the Hoylake Railway Company had obtained powers to build lines in the north of the Wirral, including in 1866 an Act for a line south to Parkgate. However, twelve years later, the company had only reached West Kirby at the Wirral's north-western corner, and so the Birkenhead Joint obtained a new Act in 1882 and built the missing 7¼ miles of single track between West Kirby and Parkgate, opened in 1886.

A second station was built at West Kirby, just east of the terminus of what had become the Wirral Railway, plus stations at Thurstaston and Heswall, and Parkgate station was enlarged to take through trains. Further stations, more like country halts, were added at Kirby Park in 1894 and Caldy in 1909. The line generally saw a service of eleven to twelve West Kirby–Hooton trains on weekdays, and four to five on Sundays up to World War II. Only occasional goods trains used the connection from the Wirral line at West Kirby before 1923, but the LMS introduced a New Brighton to Euston through coach service

11

*Hadlow Road's restored station platforms, here providing a lunch stop for walkers on the Wirral Way. (Author)*

*Another view of Hadlow Road station since restoration. The signal box, like the crossing gates, came from the ex-North Staffordshire Railway station at Hassall Green near Crewe. (Author)*

that lasted until 1939. World War II saw a great deal of increased traffic, especially for personnel at the RAF training camp at West Kirby. After 1945 usage soon dropped away, so that in the last complete year of passenger operations there were only 60,000 passenger journeys, rather than the 400,000 it was claimed were needed to make the line pay. Thurstaston and Caldy stations closed to passengers on 1st February 1954, and Kirby Park five months later, although BR was persuaded to retain two trains daily for pupils at the local boys' grammar school! This was, however, only a temporary reprieve as the whole line closed to passengers on 17th September 1956, with the last train on the 15th headed by ex-GWR class 51xx no 4122. Six years later, as if to commemorate the former joint ownership, the final freight was hauled by ex-LMS Fairburn 2-6-4T no 42229.

Since closure, the route has achieved 500,000 visitors a year, far more than it ever had as passengers! In 1969, Cheshire County Council bought the trackbed for the Wirral Country Park, the first in the country. This was officially opened on 2nd October 1973, and almost the entire route is now available to walkers, cyclists and horse riders. The line's railway remains include the former stationmasters' houses at Parkgate and Heswall, but the highlight is undoubtedly the restored station at Hadlow Road.

# Birkenhead Woodside

Modern urban and industrial development of the Wirral's eastern side began with the Chester & Birkenhead Railway. This single-track line was built north to a terminus at Grange Lane in Birkenhead, and opened in 1840 with five trains each way on weekdays and three on Sundays. Four years later it was extended to the Mersey at Monks Ferry, Merseyside's first riverside station. In 1860 the railway became the GWR/LNWR Birkenhead Joint, giving the GWR access to the Mersey. By 1876 the ferry at Woodside, more conveniently placed for Birkenhead's horse-trams, had superseded that at Monks Ferry. The railway company abandoned the latter, which, however, stayed in use as a coal depot until 1967, and built a ½ mile line, mostly in a

*Ex-LNWR Webb 2-4-2T no 6649 backs out under the bridge at the station 'throat' at Birkenhead Woodside in April 1930. (J.A.G.H. Coltas)*

*The bridge still exists, though beyond it to the right the station site is now a bus depot. (Author)*

tunnel, to a new terminal that was opened on 31st March 1878 at Woodside.

This was an imposing building with twin trainsheds, five platforms and, facing the river, the main entrance and booking hall. The latter was described as grander than those at some London termini, with lofty beams, decorated brickwork and huge sandstone fireplaces. Unfortunately entry to it was only from the ferry workshops, and so passengers used a 'temporary' side entrance into the concourse, made permanent by the arrival of the electric trams there in 1901. Despite the ferries from Liverpool, Woodside station principally served Birkenhead with GWR trains to Chester, Wrexham, Birmingham and Paddington prominent among its departures, especially once the line was quadrupled past Hooton by 1905. Services to Paddington continued into the 1960s, with six weekday through trains including an overnight sleeper in 1964. These ended in March 1967 with new schedules on the electrified West Coast Main Line at Wolverhampton. Local services to Chester and Helsby were all that were left at Woodside and the end came on 4th November 1967, with the last train the 11.38 pm two-car DMU arrival from Chester. Its route out to Rock Ferry was replaced by the former Mersey Railway electrified line from central Liverpool, and Woodside station was demolished in 1969.

# The Seacombe branch

Like Woodside, Seacombe still retains ferries across the Mersey to Liverpool, but has lost its rail link. In 1891 the Wirral Railway amalgamated with the Seacombe, Hoylake & Deeside company and began work on the latter's 3 mile Seacombe branch, originally proposed in 1863. The line opened on 1st June 1895 from Bidston to a terminus at Seacombe & Egremont, with one intermediate station at Liscard & Poulton. The line could not compete for Liverpool's commuters and mostly relied on goods traffic plus day trippers to the Wirral. The latter were particularly catered for by the 'Dodger' – a summer-season Seacombe to New Brighton service, but this only ran until 1911. In 1923 the Wirral

*The Seacombe branch line's two pre-Grouping users are represented here, with a Wirral Railway train for West Kirby on the right and a GCR Wrexham-bound one at the left. (J.F. Ward collection)*

*Despite the road traffic, the route to Seacombe still shows its railway origins in these cuttings through the sandstone rock. (Author)*

Railway became part of the LMS, which started electrifying its lines in 1936. Significantly the Seacombe branch was omitted, and its passenger service to West Kirby of 20 weekday trains each way (and almost as many on Sundays) ended with the completion of the scheme in 1938.

The LMS then concentrated on the branch's goods traffic, leaving only the LNER (formerly GCR) passenger service to Bidston and Wrexham, known as the 'Wrexham Rattler'. By 1959 this was down to thirteen trains each way on weekdays and three on Sundays. Surprisingly Seacombe's goods traffic had ended first, leaving the terminus increasingly neglected. The passenger closure proposal in 1959 included a transfer of services to nearby New Brighton and so met little opposition. The last train was the 10.20 pm arrival from Wrexham on Sunday, 3rd January 1960, which then returned empty to Bidston. The branch's last goods train ran in 1963 and since then most of the route has been used for road access to the second Mersey road tunnel.

# 2
# Liverpool's Exchange and Central Stations

*An almost deserted scene at Liverpool Central station, although the board for platform 2 gives arrivals from Nottingham, Hull (even on Sundays) and Harwich. (J.F. Ward collection)*

## Exchange station

In the late 1840s, two railways approached Liverpool from the north-east – the Lancashire & Yorkshire Railway (LYR) from Wigan and the East Lancashire Railway (ELR) from Preston. The two companies met at Walton and built a joint line into

18

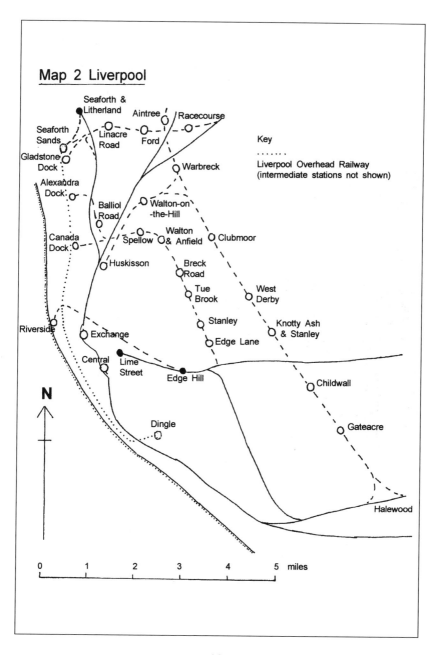

Map 2 Liverpool

Seaforth & Litherland
Aintree
Racecourse
Seaforth Sands
Linacre Road
Ford
Gladstone Dock
Alexandra Dock
Warbreck
Balliol Road
Walton-on-the-Hill
Canada Dock
Spellow
Walton & Anfield
Clubmoor
Huskisson
Breck Road
Tue Brook
West Derby
Riverside
Stanley
Knotty Ash & Stanley
Exchange
Edge Lane
Central
Lime Street
Edge Hill
Childwall
N
Dingle
Gateacre
Halewood

Key
. . . . . . .
Liverpool Overhead Railway
(intermediate stations not shown)

0    1    2    3    4    5   miles

*Ex-LMS Jubilee class 4-6-0 no 45698 'Mars' waits with the 8.10 am to Windermere at Exchange station on 12th July 1963. (J.F. Ward)*

Liverpool, but agreed on little else, not even the name of their shared terminus which was called Great Howard Street by the ELR and Borough Gaol by the LYR! By the time this station opened in 1848, the line was being extended ½ mile to a site on a viaduct above Tithebarn Street. This street name was used by the ELR for the new five-platform station opened on 13th May 1850, but the LYR preferred 'Exchange'. Inside the building, each company had its own booking office, waiting rooms and refreshment rooms. Such disputes were finally ended when the two companies amalgamated in 1859 under the title of the LYR, so that Exchange became the accepted name for the station.

The 1850 building proved inadequate for the growing LYR network, and in 1882 it was decided to replace it with a new one at street level, which was completed six years later. This had ten platforms, with the lengthy frontage of the Exchange Hotel extending either side of a four-storey entrance. The station catered not only for heavy local traffic to Southport and

20

*Exchange's magnificent frontage, now used as offices, with its entrance still clearly indicating its former function. (Author)*

21

Ormskirk (electrified by 1904 and 1913 respectively), but also for long-distance services north to Preston, Blackpool and the Lake District, and east to Manchester and Yorkshire. These continued to be busy into the 1960s, when Exchange station had the distinction of being the destination of the last steam train on a normal British Railways passenger run, on 3rd August 1968. By then, route closures, rationalisation and particularly electrification of the West Coast Main Line had led to long-distance services being concentrated at Lime Street station. In 1977 the remaining local electric trains became part of the Merseyrail system, and were diverted to an underground station at Moorfields. Exchange station finally closed on 30th April that year. The trainshed was demolished and the space used for car parking, but the frontage survived and has been restored.

# Central station

Two companies were again involved in the development of Central station, but this seems to have been harmonious and straightforward compared with the discord at Exchange. The companies at Central were the Great Northern Railway (GNR) and Manchester, Sheffield & Lincolnshire (MS&L), who were at least united in an attempt to gain traffic in a region dominated by the LNWR. To do this they backed the grouping of several small companies to form the Cheshire Lines Committee (CLC) in 1865. One of these was the Garston & Liverpool Railway, a 3 mile line from the former St Helens Railway at Garston Dock to Brunswick Dock, completed in 1864. This was intended to give the GNR and MS&L access to central Liverpool, but the new terminus was still 1½ miles away, so even before the new line opened the two companies were promoting the Liverpool Central Station Railway Act. This line, almost entirely in a tunnel, was completed to a new station on Ranelagh Street, which opened on 1st March 1874.

The new station had a single arched trainshed rising to a height of 65 ft, though this was to be outdone by the CLC's

*The Manchester, Sheffield & Lincolnshire Railway is shown among the station users in this view of Liverpool's Central station, thus dating it to the late 19th century. (J.F. Ward collection)*

*Photographed in 2003, only Lewis's department store in the background remains from the earlier view. A shopping centre occupies the station site, its Merseyrail function just about visible among its modern-day uses. (Author)*

*The last services out of Central station were DMUs to Gateacre, seen here on the last day of operations, 15th April 1972. (J.F. Ward)*

equivalent station in Manchester, opened six years later. By this time the CLC could offer the fastest journeys between the two cities, 45 minutes for the 34 miles, which was reduced to 40 minutes when the 'Straight Line' avoiding Warrington opened in 1883. This, with services to Stockport and Southport, was to remain the mainstay of the CLC services out of Central, but the links with other companies gave it routes much further afield. The two original controlling companies of the CLC, the GNR and the MS&L (Great Central from 1897), provided services from Central to the east coast ports of Hull and Harwich, and through carriages to London Marylebone. In addition, the Midland, which joined the CLC in 1866, ran through carriages to London St Pancras up to World War II. For a short spell in 1914, through non-stop expresses ran from St Pancras to Central in conjunction with the rebuilt and enlarged Adelphi Hotel.

The long-distance trains to Hull and Harwich lasted until the 1960s when they were switched to Lime Street. Local services to Southport had ended as early as 1952, those to Aintree in 1960, to

24

Stockport in 1964, and to Manchester Central in September 1966. This would have meant the closure of Central station but for trains to Gateacre on the Aintree line, which kept the station in limited use until April 1972. The station was then demolished, but its rail route south was converted for use by the electric trains of Merseyrail. The name Central is still used for the Merseyrail station below the site, from which commuters and shoppers can travel out to Southport, Ormskirk, Hunts Cross and the Wirral.

# 3
# Lines To The Docks

*The Liverpool Overhead Railway*
*Edge Hill to Riverside*
*Edge Hill to Canada and Alexandra Docks*
*The North Mersey branch*

*Ex-LMS Black Five 4-6-0 no 45313 on the approach to Riverside station on 2nd April 1960. (J.A. Peden)*

## The Liverpool Overhead Railway

This 6½ mile line, also known as the 'Overhead', the 'Ovie' or most famously as the 'Docker's Umbrella', deserves a place in any list of railway 'firsts'. Not only was it the world's first electric

26

*Lowering a span into place during the construction of the Liverpool Overhead Railway in 1892. (Author's collection)*

elevated railway, but it had the world's first railway escalator (1901) and also Britain's first automatic semaphore signals and its first colour signalling lights (1921). Such a scheme for an overhead passenger railway along the docks was first suggested in 1852, but instead horse buses were introduced on the ground-level docks goods railway. By 1877 the docks extended for over five miles along the river, and the Mersey Docks & Harbour Board (MD&HB) applied to build an elevated single-line steam railway, but this was rejected by the Board of Trade. Five years later powers were obtained for a double-track overhead railway, but nothing was done.

In 1888 the separate Liverpool Overhead Railway Company (LOR) was formed and obtained another Act. Construction began in 1889 and was completed six years later. Basically this consisted of 567 spans, each 50 ft long, on columns at a height of 16 ft above ground level. Four bridges were also required to cross wide streets and at Bramley-Moore Dock the line briefly descended to street level with gradients of 1 in 40 – a feature known locally as the 'switchback'! In 1891 the decision had been made to use electric traction, with three-car trains on a 500v dc third-rail system, running at a frequency of 2 to 10 minutes. The formal opening ceremony was on 4th February 1893, and the following month services ran from Herculaneum Dock to Alexandra Dock.

Originally there were intermediate stations for the following docks – Toxteth, Brunswick, Wapping, Princes, Clarence, Sandon, Canada and Brocklebank, with stations in the city centre at Custom House (Canning from 1945), James Street and Pier Head. The latter was the line's chief station with awnings and proper waiting rooms rather than shelters. Sandon Dock station closed in 1896, and was replaced by stations at Nelson Dock to the south and Huskisson Dock further north. The same year a station was added at Langton Dock but this only lasted until 1906. By then the route had been extended, first north to Seaforth Sands in 1894, and then south two years later over a

*A Dingle-bound train at James Street station. (W.A.C. Smith, courtesy J.F. Ward)*

28

*An LOR train crosses the lengthy bridge on the extension to Dingle in 1956. (J.F. Ward collection)*

200 ft lattice girder bridge and through a ½ mile tunnel to an underground station at Dingle.

In 1905 the LYR put in a connection to the Southport line at Seaforth & Litherland, allowing a through service from Southport to Dingle. This started in 1906 using special light-weight cars but ended with the outbreak of World War I. Also in 1906 the LYR put in a connection to the North Mersey branch allowing a Dingle–Aintree regular service, which only lasted two years. However, the link stayed in use for LOR race specials twice a year until 1940 (Grand National Friday and the preceding 'Jump Sunday'), and for the Saturday Grand Nationals from 1947 to 1956. The last addition to the stations was Gladstone Dock in 1930, but in 1940–1 the line was severely damaged by air raids, which removed two complete spans south of Canada Dock, demolished James Street station and the company's offices and caused such damage to Princes Dock station that it closed in 1946.

The line was always popular, soon reaching 8 million

passenger journeys a year (1897) and a peak of 19 million in 1919. Weekday usage was predominantly workers at the docks, factories, warehouses and offices along the route, but at weekends and bank holidays many people travelled the line for pleasure, especially in the 1930s when Round Trip tickets included a permit to visit ocean liners in the docks. There were still 10 million passengers in 1955, but the company (which was still independent) was facing a £2 million bill for renewing the line's decking. Attempts were made to sell the railway to the City Council and the MD&HB, but these were unsuccessful, so the company opted to close from Monday 31st December 1956. The last services were the previous day, with crowds using the last trains, which were timed to pass at Pier Head. From the next day only staff trains ran, but rescue attempts continued until demolition began in September 1957. This was completed by January 1959 and now the only reminders of the line are a plaque on the Mersey Tunnel ventilator building, and the entrance to the tunnel at Herculaneum.

*Dismantling the LOR at the former Huskisson Dock station in April 1958. (J.F. Ward collection)*

*The Dingle tunnel entrance still stands at Herculaneum, with 'LOR Southern Extension' and '1896' carved in the stonework above the arch. (Author)*

# Edge Hill to Riverside

Apart from the LOR, which was an independent railway built alongside all the docks, other passenger-carrying lines were constructed by 'established' railway companies to serve individual docks. Four such routes are dealt with in the rest of this chapter, with a fifth in Chapter 4. First to be built was the Liverpool & Manchester (L&M) line from Edge Hill to Waterloo, involving over two miles of double-track tunnel at a gradient of 1 in 60. This was worked by a stationary engine, which handled wagons for a goods station built across from Victoria Dock and opened in 1849.

It was another 46 years before the line saw passenger traffic. In the 1890s Liverpool was facing growing competition for the transatlantic passenger traffic from Southampton, where trains could meet liners at the quayside. At Liverpool, passengers had

Riverside Railway Station. LIVERPOOL.

*The elegant interior of Riverside station around 1910. (J. Ryan collection)*

to use horse-drawn buses from Lime Street station to the ships. As part of the improvement scheme, the LNWR (the successor to the L&M) constructed a through route at Waterloo goods station to give access to a new passenger terminal at Princes Pier. This Riverside station was built by the MD&HB with three platforms and a fine glass roof. Its opening on 12th June 1895 was timed for trains from Euston, and the arrival of Cunard's *Germanic* and departure of the same line's *Catalonia* and the White Star *Teutonic*. This set a pattern for the use of Riverside station for the next fifty years.

However, the station's usage was less than anticipated. The MD&HB set rigorous restrictions for the use of its line from Waterloo. Initially these included a man with a red flag walking in front of the boat train as it crossed the dock lines! This meant that although express boat trains from Euston might reach Edge Hill in four hours, it took another 30 minutes for the short journey to Riverside. Not surprisingly, the LYR and CLC declined to share this practice and continued to use omnibuses from Exchange and Central stations respectively, leaving

*Looking towards the site of Riverside station today. Only the memorial to ships' engine room crews at the right adds dignity to the scene. (Author)*

Riverside used only by the LNWR. Even when such restrictions were eased, weight limits meant that express locos could not reach the quay. Up to 1950, they had to be switched at Edge Hill for smaller engines, usually two per train for tackling the gradient back up from Waterloo.

So Riverside remained an anomaly – a station owned by a port authority and used by one railway company solely for boat trains. Even at its peak of ordinary services, these only averaged two trains a week although there was greater usage by troop trains during both world wars. Conventional traffic began to decrease as early as the late 1920s, when Cunard concentrated its transatlantic traffic at Southampton. The decline continued after 1945 until the whole long-distance passenger trade was ended by the increased use of air transport. Trains to Riverside were down to only two a month by the early 1970s and the last train left on 25th February 1971. This was a troop special for servicemen returning from Northern Ireland; four days later the station closed. Its buildings were used by the Isle of Man steamer company and for storage of the Merseyside Museum's Large Objects Collection, including road vehicles, but have since been demolished.

# Edge Hill to Canada and Alexandra Docks

As Liverpool's docks extended north along the Mersey, the LNWR added a further branch north-west to Bootle from Edge Hill. Goods trains ran as far as the first station, Stanley, in June 1866 and to Canada Dock four months later. Passenger services were similarly added in stages, first to Tue Brook, then to Breck Road, Walton & Anfield and Canada Dock by July 1870. An extra station was added at Edge Lane in November 1870 and more importantly in 1880 a 'satellite' branch was opened to Atlantic

*The railtour visit to Alexandra Dock station in 1959. (G. Harrop)*

*The line's freight workings (which still continue) are shown by an ex-LNWR class G2 0-8-0 hauling wagons out of Breck Road sidings in 1950. (J. Gahan)*

Dock, initially for goods traffic and then for passenger trains to the terminus, renamed Alexandra Dock for the opening service on 1st September 1881. Balliol Road station was also opened on this branch and a final intermediate station on the 'main' line added at Spellow the following year.

The dock railways system was often linked to other lines to provide through routes. In this case a connection was put in at Bootle Junction between the Alexandra Dock branch and the adjacent LYR Liverpool–Southport line, allowing the LNWR to run its trains to Southport from Edge Hill. These began on 1st May 1886 and included through carriages for Euston for many years. In 1966 a through DMU service was put on between Liverpool Lime Street and Southport, which lasted until 1977. It well outlived the docks passenger traffic, which ended to Canada Dock as early as 1941 due to air raid damage. Alexandra Dock and the other stations on the branch lasted another seven years, closing 'temporarily' on 31st May 1948, but this was made permanent the following year. The two dock stations were almost intact at a railtour visit in 1959, but were later demolished. Some remains of other stations survive – platforms at Walton & Anfield, Balliol Road's booking hall and Spellow's station building, latterly used as a bookmaker's! Except for the Canada Dock section, the line is still in use for goods traffic from Seaforth Dock, and has been suggested for part of the proposed Central Railway route to the Channel Tunnel.

# The North Mersey branch

Of all the dock railways considered here, this was the least likely to carry passenger traffic. It was completed without stations by the LYR in 1867, as a freight route between its North Mersey goods yard and the Liverpool–Wigan line at Fazakerley. A rudimentary racecourse station was provided at Aintree Cinder Lane around 1890, but it was another 16 years before regular passenger services were introduced as part of the LYR suburban electrification. This scheme included a link between Sefton Junction and Mersey Branch Junction, allowing the line to be used for a Liverpool Exchange–Aintree service. This began on 1st June 1906, with stops at stations newly provided on the branch at Linacre Road and Ford. A single-platform station was added at Gladstone Dock in 1914 but was only in use for ten years. In 1922, there had been seven weekday trains to Gladstone Dock and sixteen to Exchange (nine on Sundays), but by 1950 there were only five trains a day, and the service was withdrawn on 2nd April 1951 when Linacre Road and Ford stations closed.

The racecourse station, officially called Racecourse from 1910, lingered on until 1962. It was only used at the Grand National meeting, for LOR trains (up to 1956) as well as LYR specials, and was unusual in that it didn't have proper platforms. Instead the eastbound trackbed was raised to act as a solitary platform for passengers whose raceday trains arrived and departed on the westbound track – no 'normal' traffic being allowed on the eastbound track on those days! Nothing remains at the station

*Raceday crowds cross the eastbound track at Aintree Racecourse station from a train headed by one of the LYR's 4-4-2 Atlantic engines in 1913. (Stations UK)*

*A more workaday scene in 1934 at the ex-LYR Aintree engine shed close to the line, with an appropriate loco – LYR class 6F 0-8-0 no 12726. (F. Dean)*

*A final reminder of Liverpool's once-extensive docks traffic – ex-LMS class 3F (Jinty) no 47404 and ex-LNWR class G2 no 49437 haul a passenger train at Waterloo in 1958. (J.A. Peden)*

site, nor at the other stations, except for platform supports at Linacre Road. Most of the route went out of use in 1972 and is now a path from the once-extensive sidings east of the racecourse, through housing developments (including Red Rum Close!) and across the bridge over the A59 to the Liverpool Loop Line Path (see next chapter). Beyond this a single track is still in place passing the sites of the LYR Aintree engine shed and Ford and Linacre Road stations, but is now little used although it was repaired for use by engineering trains in October 2002.

# 4
# The CLC North Liverpool Line

## Halewood to Aintree and Huskisson

*The last scheduled passenger train over the ex-CLC line north of Gateacre at Aintree Central on 5th April 1960, with Fairburn class 4P 2-6-4T no 42113. (J.F. Ward)*

The original 1864 terminus for the CLC at Brunswick Dock was not only badly placed for Liverpool city centre, it was also left in the wrong place for freight as the city's port traffic moved north along the Mersey. Thus in 1873 a 23 acre site was acquired close to Huskisson Dock north of the centre. The site was only 1½ miles from Central station but the cost of tunnelling under the

*The Liverpool Loop Line Path uses two steel lattice-girder bridges built in the 1930s; this one is over the East Lancs Road. (Author)*

city centre was prohibitive, and so the CLC decided to build a line north from a triangular junction at Halewood around the east of Liverpool to stations at Aintree and Walton-on-the-Hill. This opened for freight and passenger services from Liverpool Central on 1st December 1879, with intermediate stations at Gateacre (for Woolton), Childwall, Old Swan & Knotty Ash (Knotty Ash & Stanley from 1888) and West Derby. The extension from Walton to Huskisson opened in 1880, for goods in July and passenger services in August. These only lasted until 1885, and to Walton-on-the-Hill until 1918, though the branch remained in use for freight and for access to the engine shed at Walton.

The line's importance was increased for freight by Midland links to Sandon Dock in 1882 and to Alexandra Dock three years later, and for passengers by the Southport & Cheshire Lines

*West Derby station building is the only one to survive on the line, with its booking office in use as 'The Old Gas Station' when photographed in 2003! (Author)*

*Walton-on-the-Hill station platforms were still visible in 1971, although not in regular use since 1918. The tunnel ahead led towards Huskisson. (J.F. Ward)*

*Gateacre station around 1907, looking towards Halewood and clearly showing the distinctive edging to the canopies. (J.F. Ward collection)*

Extension from Aintree to Southport, opened in 1884. New passenger stations were opened at Clubmoor in 1927 and at Warbreck two years later, but Childwall closed in 1931. The line had been built with provision for four tracks, but two were all that were needed even before passenger traffic began to fall away after 1945.

John Ward has lived most of his life close to the line and remembers when it was still busy in the summer of 1948. As a youngster he was befriended by the signalman at Gateacre and was allowed into the signal box with its magical array of bells and levers. Under supervision he was sometimes allowed to pull the levers, not an easy task as some of them controlled signals as far away as 300 yards. John could listen to the signalman's conversations with adjacent boxes and read the entries in the train book, always remembering to keep out of sight when a train passed in case he was spotted by the driver or guard. On fine evenings a game of cricket in the nearby goods yard could be interrupted by a bell and a quick sprint by the signalman back to his box!

The extension from Aintree to Southport was the first to close, in 1952, while the section from Gateacre to Aintree lost its regular passenger traffic eight years later. Aintree, however, kept its Grand National specials until 1963. These had long been an important feature of the line's passenger activity – as early as 1905 there were 29 special trains for the race meeting to Aintree's CLC station alone. Around 30 were recorded each year from 1928 to 1939, the highlight being the through working from London King's Cross. Postwar usage never returned to these levels, although there were nine long-distance specials each year from 1951 to 1959, dropping to six for the final years to 1963. In the penultimate year, 1962, these included trains travelling north-wards over the line to Aintree Central (as it was known after nationalisation) from Luton, Hull, King's Norton (Birmingham) and Cleethorpes. The Halewood to Gateacre section was the last to see regular passenger trains (from Liverpool Central) until these finished on 15th April 1972.

*Grand National excursions over the ex-CLC line continued until 1963, although this scene is in 1959, with the former Brighton Belle observation car at the rear of a special from Cleethorpes. (J.A. Peden)*

Freight was always important on the line, especially to and from the docks. As early as 1898 there was a regular daily goods working to King's Cross. By 1939 Huskisson alone had twenty daily booked freight departures, with eighteen in 1954 including three to York (this working saw ex-LNER Gresley-designed V2 locos for a time in the early 1960s). Interesting workings from Walton shed included a daily anhydrite train returning empty to Long Meg in Cumbria from Widnes chemical works, and one to Colwick (Nottingham) believed to be carrying imported tobacco. Goods traffic finished at Aintree in 1964 but lasted longer to the docks, the ex-Midland branches to Sandon and Alexandra Docks being the first to close in 1968. Freight services to the 'main' line stations ended with the closure of Knotty Ash goods depot in 1972 but lingered to Huskisson – by then using a single track – until the mid 1970s. In 1987, work started on converting the trackbed from Halewood to Aintree into a path for walkers and cyclists, now open for 8½ miles as the Liverpool Loop Line Path, part of the Trans Pennine Trail. Passing through largely built-up areas, this route has not been without its problems and in 2003 extra police patrols were mounted to reduce crime during the school summer and October half-term holidays!

# 5
# Out From St Helens And Wigan

*The St Helens Railway*
*The Wigan Junction Railway*
*St Helens to Lowton St Mary's*

*Stanier 4P no 42647 leaving Wigan Central in 1964, the year the station closed. (R. Hunt collection)*

## The St Helens Railway

This early line, completed in 1833, was typical of such lines in that it was intended for the movement of freight, with passengers

45

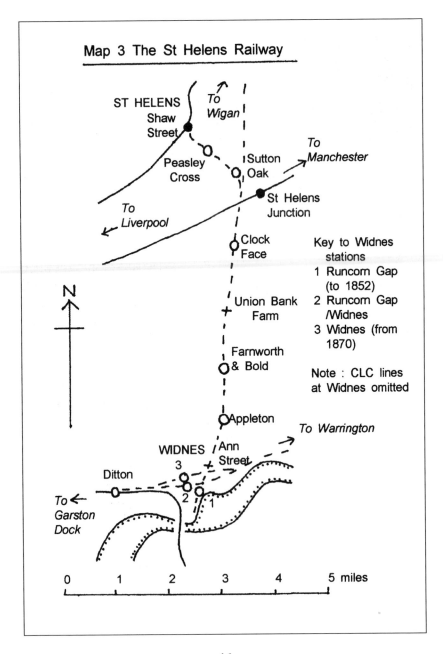

Map 3 The St Helens Railway

ST HELENS
Shaw
Street

To
Wigan

Peasley
Cross

Sutton
Oak

To
Manchester

St Helens
Junction

To
Liverpool

Clock
Face

Key to Widnes
stations
1 Runcorn Gap
(to 1852)
2 Runcorn Gap
/Widnes
3 Widnes (from
1870)

N

Union Bank
Farm

Farnworth
& Bold

Note : CLC lines
at Widnes omitted

Appleton

To Warrington

WIDNES /Ann
3     Street
Ditton

To ←
Garston
Dock

2    1

0    1    2    3    4    5 miles

*The pit for the turning mechanism for the line's swing bridge over the Sankey Canal at Widnes, with the site of the original Runcorn Gap station in the right background. (Author)*

as an afterthought, and was built along the lines of a canal. Thus there were level stretches, with inclines worked by stationary engines replacing flights of locks. The railway was built to move coal from mines in the St Helens area to a dock at Runcorn Gap on the Mersey estuary, in competition with the Sankey Brook Navigation. This was the first English canal and was opened in 1757 and extended in 1833 (the same year as the railway) to Runcorn Gap. The railway took a more direct route from Peasley Cross south of St Helens, using an incline to climb to the Liverpool & Manchester line, which was crossed by an iron bridge. A second incline was built for the steepest part of the descent down to present-day Widnes. The line was first used by a coal train in November 1832, but at the official opening on 21st February 1833 it was still unfinished, chiefly the inclines and the dock. Passenger operations of a kind did take place, but details are sketchy – initially perhaps two trains a day taking

47

three hours for the 8 mile journey, with passengers required to walk the two inclines!

The railway's potentially ruinous battle with the canal for the coal-carrying trade lasted until 1845, when they combined as the St Helens Canal & Railway Company. Over the next few years, the inclines were replaced by easier gradients for locomotive working and a double track was laid. A replacement station was built at St Helens, with new ones at Appleton, Farnworth (Farnworth & Bold from 1890) and Sutton (Sutton Oak from 1864). There were later additions at Bold (only open 1853–8), Clock Face and Peasley Cross. The elimination of the inclines reduced the St Helens–Runcorn Gap journey time to 25 minutes, and passenger numbers increased from 26,000 in 1838 to 260,000 in 1850. In 1852 the company expanded west to Garston Dock, and east to Warrington a year later. A new Runcorn Gap station was built closer to the fast-growing town of Widnes, and the St Helens service increased to twelve trains each way on weekdays, with four on Sundays. The LNWR absorbed the St Helens

*Appleton station, looking south towards the factory chimneys of Widnes in 1947. (Stations UK)*

48

*A Webb 'Cauliflower' 0-6-0 heads north with a goods train through Farnworth & Bold station in LNWR days. (J. Ryan collection)*

Railway in 1864, and decided to remove both road and rail crossings on the level in Widnes. Thus in 1869 a 1¼ mile deviation line was opened for the 1852–3 east–west route, bridging the St Helens line and including a spur to it. The second Runcorn Gap station, which had been called Widnes since 1864, closed in 1870 and was replaced by a new Widnes station on the deviation line.

By 1900 the LNWR was operating a service of nine weekday trains (three on Sundays) from St Helens to Ditton Junction on the 1852 Garston Dock line, 1½ miles west of Widnes. Two halts were opened in 1911 at Ann Street (Widnes) and Union Bank Farm for the introduction of a short-lived steam railmotor service, the line soon reverting to push-pull operation using Webb 2-4-2 tank engines which stayed in use up to the end of passenger services in 1951. By then the 'Ditton Dodger' service consisted of three morning and three late-afternoon trains Mondays–Fridays, with five more evenly spread on Saturdays, and no trains on Sundays. The final train was the 5.56 pm from

St Helens to Ditton Junction on Saturday, 16th June 1951, though St Helens Shaw Street–St Helens Junction services continued to use the northern part of the line until 1965. The line remained in use for freight and diversions, but was singled in 1969 between Farnworth and Sutton Oak, where the engine shed effectively shut at that time. In 1981 the line closed as a through route, and five years later it was reduced to a 1 mile siding to works south of St Helens with an occasional freight train right up to September 2002.

Little is left of the line, especially at the Widnes end where the docks area has been landscaped, removing all traces of the once-numerous sidings. To the north, 2¼ miles of the route have been used for the A557 bypass around Widnes but as this swings west to the M62, 3½ miles of former trackbed are still visible. This can be walked – with some difficulty through areas of undergrowth, flooded patches and much loose ballast – past the sites of Union Bank Farm halt and the stations at Clock Face and Sutton Oak,

*Ex-LNWR Webb 2-4-2T no 6628 at Sutton Oak engine shed. A similar loco hauled the last St Helens–Ditton Junction train over the line on 16th June 1951. (J. Davenport)*

*The last surviving section of the St Helens Railway was this siding heading right, with the site of Sutton Oak station on the cleared stretch towards the top left. (Author)*

where nothing remains. In 2003 the final mile into St Helens was a rusting single-track branch line, all that is left of this historic railway.

# The Wigan Junction Railway

Perhaps surprisingly, from 1923 to 1948 the LNER ran trains into Wigan. The origin of this was the Wigan Junction Railway (WJR), promoted by the CLC in 1874 for access to this area of the Lancashire coalfield. However, only the MS&L of the three controlling companies stayed involved, and effectively ran the line. It was built from Glazebrook on the CLC Manchester–Liverpool line to a temporary terminus at Strangeways Hall Colliery, two miles from Wigan, and opened for goods and

51

## Map 4 Greater Manchester

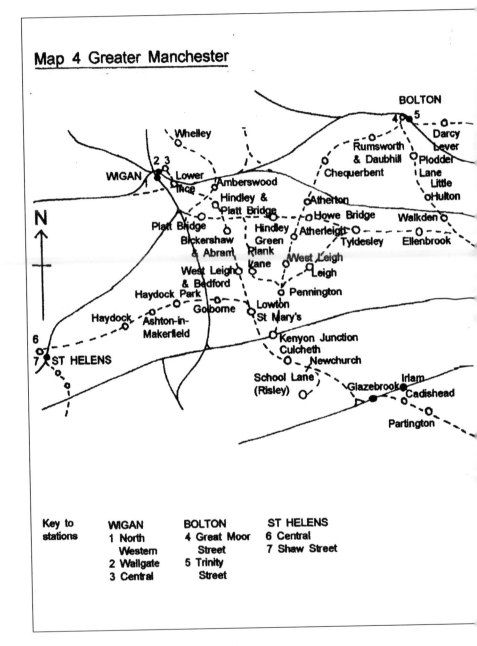

| Key to stations | WIGAN | BOLTON | ST HELENS |
|---|---|---|---|
| | 1 North Western | 4 Great Moor Street | 6 Central |
| | 2 Wallgate | 5 Trinity Street | 7 Shaw Street |
| | 3 Central | | |

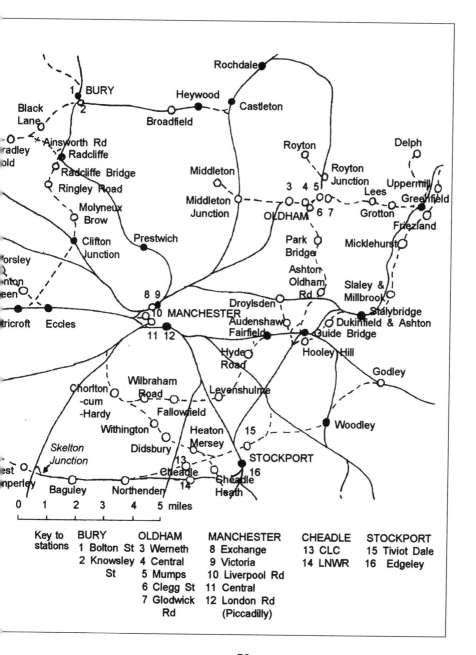

Key to stations

| | BURY | OLDHAM | MANCHESTER | CHEADLE | STOCKPORT |
|---|---|---|---|---|---|
| | 1 Bolton St | 3 Werneth | 8 Exchange | 13 CLC | 15 Tiviot Dale |
| | 2 Knowsley St | 4 Central | 9 Victoria | 14 LNWR | 16 Edgeley |
| | | 5 Mumps | 10 Liverpool Rd | | |
| | | 6 Clegg St | 11 Central | | |
| | | 7 Glodwick Rd | 12 London Rd (Piccadilly) | | |

*Staff involved in the construction of Wigan Central assembled for this photograph taken before the opening of the station in 1892. (R. Hunt collection)*

mineral traffic in 1879. Five years later passenger services began, calling at stations at Culcheth, Lowton St Mary's, Plank Lane for West Leigh (West Leigh & Bedford from 1894), Bickershaw & Abram, Strangeways & Hindley (Hindley & Platt Bridge 1892-1950, then Hindley South) and Lower Ince, before a terminus in Darlington Street, Wigan. The MS&L had hopes of an extension to a crossing of the Ribble and access to Blackpool, but all that was built was a ½ mile line to a new terminus in Wigan, named Central station and opened in 1892.

Trains to Blackpool did run over a short section of the line, but these were LNWR and later LMS services. In 1886 the LNWR opened a connection from the Wigan–Eccles line which after ½ mile of WJR rails joined the Whelley Loop (see next chapter). This route was used by the Manchester Exchange–Windermere residential express with Club carriages, and by Blackpool excursions from Sheffield and the East Midlands until well into

*Passengers wait at a neat and tidy Culcheth station in the early 1960s. (G. Harrop)*

the 1950s. Everyday services over the WJR were more mundane. In 1903, for example, the Great Central (the name used by the MS&L from 1897) ran eight trains on Mondays to Fridays to Manchester Central and six to Warrington, using a north-west curve opened at Glazebrook by the CLC in 1900. There was an extra train to Manchester on Saturdays but the five Sunday trains ran only to Glazebrook. In 1923 the Great Central became part of the LNER, which thus gained access to Wigan, though by a rather neglected and rundown line. Retired railwayman Stanley Morris started as a cleaner aged 18 in 1925 at Lower Ince engine shed, mostly working on ex-GCR J10 locos. He particularly remembers the morning run to Manchester Central, when the passengers formed an audience of salivating commuters as delicious smells rose into the morning air. These were from bacon, eggs and fried bread cooking on the fireman's shovel, cleaned previously using the engine's steam injector.

Services increased for a time with the development of two major industrial sites to the south-east of Wigan. Since 1910 iron

*Engine shed staff with an ex-GCR J10 loco at Lower Ince in the late 1920s –
Stanley Morris at the top right. (Courtesy S. Morris/N. Cain)*

*Wigan Central after closure in 1964. Only the building at the left had remained railway premises up to then – the more imposing structure at the right had been used as a bathroom showroom! (R. Hunt collection)*

and steel had been made at Irlam, 1½ miles east of Glazebrook on the CLC main line. During the 1930s the works were expanded, and workers' trains ran from Wigan, including the day's first departure. At the outbreak of World War II, a halt was added on the ex-WJR line at Newchurch east of Culcheth to serve a nearby camp for the navy's Air Electrical School. From the halt, a 1½ mile single-track branch was constructed to a new station, School Lane, at the huge Royal Ordnance Factory at Risley. Many of this works' total of 30,000 employees lived on site, but others travelled daily on more workers' trains from Wigan.

After 1945, the line went into terminal decline and was an obvious candidate to be a Beeching closure. The withdrawal of passenger services came on 2nd November 1964, with freight ending in stages to 1968. Now there is almost nothing to show that this railway ever existed in Wigan. To the south, some landscaped sections remain at Ince, and short stretches can be walked near Pennington Flash. The clearest remains are near Culcheth, where 1½ miles of trackbed heading south-east through the station site are now walkable as the Culcheth Linear Park. A further ½ mile can sometimes be walked, but the path is not maintained and is often flooded. It leads to the site of Newchurch halt, where steps remain. Past this, the rest of the route to Glazebrook has now returned to farmland.

# St Helens to Lowton St Mary's

As well as attempting to reach Blackpool via Wigan, the MS&L was behind a plan to link St Helens with Southport and the North Liverpool docks. Nothing came of this scheme except the first 8 miles from Lowton St Mary's on the WJR into St Helens.

*Ex-LMS Fowler class 4F 0-6-0 no 44501 heads a railtour to St Helens Central in 1963, eleven years after the station closed to regular passenger traffic. (B.G. Barlow, courtesy J.A. Peden)*

*Haydock station, seen soon after closure in 1952, had few facilities for eastbound passengers and none at all for anyone travelling to St Helens. (J.A. Peden collection)*

This was authorised as the St Helens & Wigan Junction Railway in 1885, but even a name change to the Liverpool, St Helens & South Lancashire Railway in 1889 didn't speed things up, as it was another six years before any of the line was open. Even then it was only for goods and half the line was still single track. A second line was added for the start of passenger services, but the last 200 yards into St Helens stayed a single track over a costly viaduct. The first passenger train ran to the races at Haydock Park in February 1899, but it was the following year before a full service was begun, starting with an opening ceremony on 2nd January 1900 attended by 300 guests including the local MP and the Mayor of St Helens. The public service began the next day with six weekday trains each way between St Helens Central and stations at Haydock, Ashton-in-Maker-field, Golborne (Golborne North after nationalisation) and Lowton St Mary's, with usually a connection required for Glazebrook and Manchester Central.

59

*Racegoers at Haydock Park station at least had a substantial footbridge, which has survived demolition if not the graffiti-writers! (Author)*

The company had only six years of 'independence' as, like the WJR, it was taken over in 1906 by the Great Central (as the MS&L was known from 1897). The service was maintained but little was done to encourage passengers at St Helens Central, where trains arrived at a single wooden platform with a small shelter. The LNER, which took over the line at the Grouping of 1923, ran more trains from Manchester Central into St Helens, with Wigan in the 1930s chiefly reached by a railcar shuttle service from Lowton. However, the St Helens line did not long survive nationalisation in 1948 as the passenger service, by then down to three trains a day, was withdrawn on 3rd March 1952, little more than fifty years after it began. Colliery traffic and racecourse specials to Haydock Park continued for another dozen years, but the line finally closed in 1965, with small sections staying in use for industry; in 1968 a connection was put in from Golborne Junction on the West Coast Main Line to an oil storage depot at Haydock, using 2½ miles of the St Helens branch. This went out of use in the 1980s, but even in 2003 a tiny section still had regular freight trains. The main line link was used twice a week for tar trains travelling 500 yards onto the former branch before reversing into the works. Elsewhere little remains of the line, particularly in St Helens where the route has been completely lost. Short stretches can be walked at Haydock, but in general this line has disappeared.

# 6
# More Lines Around Wigan

*The Whelley Loop*
*Wigan to Eccles*
*Tyldesley–Leigh–Pennington*
*Pennington to Platt Bridge*

*Near Hindley, a closed colliery branch from the Pennington–Platt Bridge line crosses the former WJR trackbed, with beyond it the bridge for the also-closed Wigan–Eccles line. (Author)*

## The Whelley Loop

This was originally built to allow trains to bypass Wigan as part of the Lancashire Union Railway (LUR) route from Blackburn to

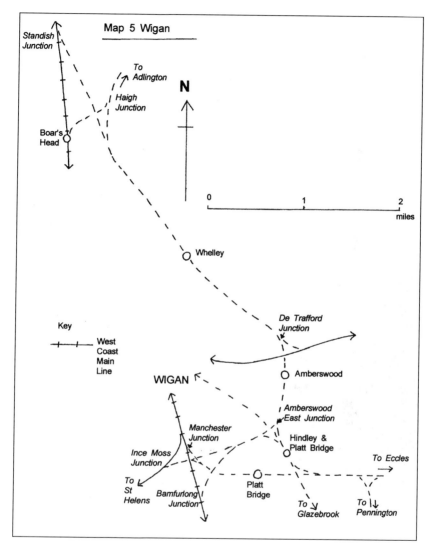

St Helens. Heading off from that company's Adlington–Boar's Head line at Haigh Junction, the loop went through the Haigh Hall estates using a cut-and-cover tunnel, which was replaced by a cutting in 1883–4. It then passed coal mines and iron works by the Leeds and Liverpool Canal and swung west to the LUR

*Whelley was the site of a short-lived station used only in 1872 but its stationmaster's house was still standing in this 1964 view. (J.A. Peden collection)*

Wigan–St Helens line at Ince Moss Junction. The line was opened in 1869, primarily for freight, although in January 1872 the LNWR opened stations at Whelley and Amberswood for a passenger service of three trains a day to Liverpool. This only lasted two months; the stations closed in March 1872 and never reopened, though the station house remained at Whelley for almost the next century.

In 1882 the line was extended north to the West Coast Main Line at Standish Junction, and four years later to the same line south of Wigan at Bamfurlong Junction. This created an alternative north-south route, much used by freight trains. Further connections added to the usefulness of the loop, starting with a link to the LYR Wigan–Hindley–Manchester route at De Trafford Junction, built with the LUR line in 1869. At Amberswood East Junction a connection was provided to the Wigan Junction Railway in 1880, which was extended to the LNWR Wigan–Eccles–Manchester line in 1886. These

*This scene with locally-built 0-6-0T 'Manton' in 1908 at Alexandra Pit close to the line typifies the industrial activity along the Whelley Loop (Author's collection)*

allowed passenger trains from Manchester to Blackpool and Windermere (including the famous Club trains – see Chapter 11) to avoid the congestion at Wigan.

The Whelley Loop remained busy for diversions, freight, holiday traffic and some regular passenger services well into the 1960s, and was particularly well used during the electrification of the West Coast Main Line around 1970. Upon completion of this in 1972, the line was singled and went out of use during 1976. Two years later, there were proposals to relay the track to reinstate the Whelley Loop as a Wigan railway 'bypass', but these came to nothing.

The northern end of the route has been lost, including the connections to the main line and former Adlington–Boar's Head line. However, an imposing viaduct over the river Douglas still stands though almost hidden in vegetation. Through the Haigh Hall estate the line becomes walkable, and the path continues past the sites of the short-lived Whelley and Amberswood stations. It then skirts a flooded area on Ince Moss before

65

*The thirteen arches and six steel spans of the line's viaduct still cross the Douglas valley. (Author)*

regaining the trackbed as far as the A573, just east of the present-day main line.

# Wigan to Eccles

During the 19th century, there was fierce competition between the LNWR and the LYR in the coalfield area between Wigan and Manchester. Three of the four main links between the two centres are still in use, the one that has not survived being the LNWR Wigan–Eccles line. The LNWR already had one route from Manchester to Wigan, using the 1830 Liverpool & Manchester line to Parkside and the 1832 Wigan Branch Railway. However, this was a roundabout route, and in 1864 a new line was opened from Wigan to Eccles on the former L&M route into Manchester. Although more direct, connections

*Stanier 4P no 2539 heads a three-coach Manchester train through Tyldesley. (W.D. Cooper)*

with six other lines, plus colliery branches, made for a very complex pattern of workings.

The route left the West Coast Main Line at Manchester Junction, south of Wigan. Almost immediately there was a branch from the LUR Wigan–St Helens line, before the first station at Platt Bridge. Then a curve came in from the Wigan Junction Railway of 1879, allowing access to and from the Whelley Loop at Amberswood. Next was a triangular junction with the LNWR line to Pennington, followed by Hindley Green station. This, like most on the line, was a timber construction, but was particularly well looked after, winning awards for best-kept station in its area between 1947 and 1952. At Howe Bridge, junctions allowed trains from Bolton to join the line both westbound and eastbound, just before the station, called Chowbent until 1901. Although it was the first to close, this had been a busy station up to the early 1950s with sometimes as many as 500 people departing on Saturday morning holiday specials. There was no access from Leigh here, this came 1½ miles later at

Tyldesley with the branch to Pennington, built at the same time as the Wigan–Eccles line.

Tyldesley was the largest town served by the line and boasted its 'premier' station. For many years it was famous as a starting point for pigeon races. The town is built on the first rising ground from the Cheshire Plain to the south, which gave it the nickname 'Bongs' (from 'banks'). On certain summer Fridays, baskets of racing pigeons would arrive by train at the station, ready for release by the porters at 11 am sharp the next day. Not all of them got further than Gin Pits, just south of the station, where shotgun blasts reduced the numbers flying overhead! The next station was Ellenbrook, before the line from Bolton Great Moor Street (completed in 1875) joined at Roe Green Junction. Worsley was not the most important station on the line, but it was certainly the most elaborate, built in brick with an elegant glazed canopy. It was once described as 'a shining jewel in the crown of the LNWR'. Near here the Earl of Ellesmere had cut the first sod for the line in 1861, and his support for the line from his seat at

*Tyldesley station with a railtour visit in 1966, headed by Black Five no 45154 'Lanarkshire Yeomanry'. (Author's collection)*

*Something of the splendour of Worsley station in Edwardian days can be seen here. (Author's collection)*

*Today only platform remnants and the trackbed are left from the earlier scene at Worsley. (Author)*

nearby Worsley Hall surely accounted for the palatial nature of the station. One more station was built before the junction at Eccles, at Monton Green, added in 1887 as the residential area grew.

In its heyday, the line must have been year-round one of the busiest in the region. As well as local traffic, there were expresses from Manchester to Blackpool, Windermere, Edinburgh and Glasgow, either via Wigan or using the Whelley Loop. Perhaps the start of its decline came with the absorption of the LYR by the LNWR, shortly before the grouping of 1923. This gave the newly formed LMS other options using the former LYR routes, which both ran through and bypassed Bolton. By World War II, for

*The last regular passenger trains at Tyldesley were DMUs running between Manchester and Liverpool via Leigh. (Tyldesley Historical Society)*

70

example, the Windermere expresses had been switched to the LYR direct line. This pattern continued after 1945, and by 'Beeching' a case could be made that this was a surplus line whose remaining traffic could be transferred elsewhere. Howe Bridge station had closed in 1959, and Ellenbrook, Hindley Green and Platt Bridge two years later, so only users of Tyldesley, Worsley and Monton Green were left to protest against final closure. The Tyldesley–Wigan section closed to regular passenger traffic on 2nd November 1964, although the line west to Wigan was still used for summer holiday workings until 1968. The Tyldesley–Eccles section shut with the line to Leigh on 5th May 1969.

Up to 2003, the first two miles of the line east from Wigan retained a single track, which had served the colliery at Bickershaw (Leigh), closed in 1992. From Bickershaw West Junction through Hindley Green and Tyldesley, the trackbed is mostly intact and unofficially walkable. There are gaps, for example at Howe Bridge, and as the track has not been maintained, it is impassable in places. The situation improves, at least for the walker, at Ellenbrook where the footpath becomes official as one of Salford's 'Looplines'. Thus the 4½ miles to the site of Monton Green station are in reasonable condition (from there to Eccles the route has been built over). However, in January 2002 there were proposals that the Leigh–Tyldesley–Ellenbrook section could be used as part of a £26 million guided busway scheme for access to Manchester. It was suggested that restoring the rail link would make more sense!

# Tyldesley–Leigh–Pennington

This line was built by the LNWR in conjunction with the Wigan–Eccles route and opened on the same date – 1st September 1864. Leaving the direct line 350 yards west of Tyldesley station, it ran through the coal-mining and cotton-manufacturing town of Leigh to reach the former Kenyon & Leigh Junction Railway at Bradshaw Leach (later Pennington). Its only station was at Leigh and was called Bedford Leigh until 1876, then Leigh & Bedford

*Pennington station looking towards Kenyon Junction in 1912, when the main focus of interest was the garden! (J. Ryan collection)*

*The same location photographed in 2003 shows a very different transport scene, with the A579 Leigh bypass now occupying the course of the former railway. (Author)*

until 1914 when it became simply Leigh. By this time the original station, described as a 'spartan affair', had been replaced by a substantial timber construction with roof ironwork supporting a timber and glass canopy. The main passenger service was from Manchester to Leigh via Tyldesley, comprising fifteen weekday trains in 1934, including some through to Kenyon Junction and Liverpool. By the 1960s the line was much used for Liverpool Lime Street to Manchester Exchange trains, some continuing as TransPennine services to Leeds and Hull. It was particularly busy for Leigh's Wakes Week holidays, beginning the first weekend in July. In 1958 for example, eight special trains left on the Friday evening and Saturday for Morecambe, Blackpool, Fleetwood, North Wales and Devon. Despite surviving the closure of the route west of Tyldesley in January 1968, the end for the line came only 17 months later. The last day of operations, 3rd May 1969, saw Leigh station packed once more as crowds gathered for special trains to Blackpool. When these returned in the evening, the station closed and demolition began later that year. With the reconnection of Mansfield to the rail network, Leigh is now the largest town in England without a rail service.

# Pennington to Platt Bridge

This 3½ mile line was built by the LNWR to keep the rival Wigan Junction Railway (WJR) out of a productive area of the Lancashire Coalfield. Construction started in 1883 and goods traffic began two years later. Passenger services were not considered, until in 1896 a further Act authorised the construction of an avoiding line or flyover at Pennington to allow a Leigh–Wigan service. An intermediate station was built at Plank Lane ('Plonk Lone' to the locals), not to be confused with the WJR's similarly named station, which was renamed West Leigh & Bedford. At 6.43 am on 1st October 1903, the first Wigan train left Leigh with one passenger – probably a fair indication of the lack of demand for this service. At least there were more 'customers' the next year, when Buffalo Bill's Wild West Show arrived at Pennington using three special trains reportedly

*Ex-LNWR class 7F 0-8-0 no 49149 hauling colliery wagons at Pennington in 1954. (Author's collection)*

carrying 500 horses, and 800 artistes and their assistants. More usual services were a couple of Leigh–Wigan trains each weekday, and one daily Manchester–Blackpool train each way. This service continued until around 1930, outlasting Plank Lane station, which closed on 22nd February 1915.

The Leigh–Wigan service lingered until 1942, after which the line continued in use for freight trains (especially carrying coal), ballast workings and holiday specials from Leigh and Tyldesley until 1953. By this time using the route west of Pennington must have been quite an experience, as the line had to cross Pennington Flash – a large 'lagoon' caused by flooding due to mining subsidence (six separate seams of coal had been mined in the area). Despite repairs to the embankment by Italian prisoners of war during World War II, trains soon after were little above water level and the line south of Bickershaw Colliery was abandoned after an LCGB special in 1963 crossed stretches under water! However, north of the mine a single track was retained for

74

*Hunslet 0-6-0ST 'Warrior' at work at Bickershaw Colliery in the late 1970s – one of the last uses of steam locos in industrial South Lancashire. (R. Lees)*

the colliery, hence the 'lost train' story of 1971. Apparently a coal train heading north from Bickershaw found a parcels and Royal Mail train southbound on the single line, 'lost' since Wigan and facing a lengthy reversal to get off the colliery branch. A few more legitimate specials ventured onto the line in its final years, the last being an 'Institute of Mining Engineers' charter in September 1991. Six months later, Bickershaw Colliery closed and the branch went out of use, although a single rusting track still led from the former Wigan–Eccles line down towards the colliery site for the next eleven years. Much of the route on towards Pennington was buried under mining waste, but a short stretch of embankment can be seen in Pennington Flash.

# 7
# Bolton And Bury

*Bolton to Kenyon Junction*
*Roe Green Junction to Bolton*
*Clifton Junction to Bury*
*Bolton–Bury–Rochdale*

*Ex-LYR 2-4-2T no 50829 at Bury Knowsley Street station in August 1953.*
*(J. Davenport)*

## Bolton to Kenyon Junction

Despite the fame of George Stephenson's Liverpool & Manchester Railway (L&M), it was not the first public railway in NW England. That was the Bolton & Leigh Railway, the first three

76

miles of which opened two years earlier in 1828. Construction had begun in 1825, with George Stephenson as the engineer in charge. Like the St Helens Railway, it was designed with relatively level stretches separated by inclines. The Bolton end constituted one of the 'levels', with branches to a foundry and warehouse on Deansgate, and to a coal yard on Great Moor Street. Next was the first incline, at Daubhill, with a 20hp stationary engine hauling wagons ¾ mile up gradients as steep as 1 in 33. After almost 2 miles on the level, a second similar but longer incline at Chequerbent, worked by a 50hp engine, took the line down to a final level stretch at Leigh.

The opening ceremony took place on 1st August 1828, with a journey from collieries near the top of the Chequerbent incline to the coal yard in Bolton. A 'coach' was provided for the coal-owners and their guests, plus thirteen wagons for others, all hauled initially by Robert Stephenson's *Lancashire Witch*. This was only to the top of Daubhill incline; it was intended that horses would pull the train from the foot of the incline into Bolton, but they were replaced by some of the vast crowd of onlookers, estimated at 40,000. The 7¾ mile single-track line fully opened to Leigh in March 1830, but there were no passenger services until 1831, when an excursion from Bolton to Newton Races is recorded for 2nd June. By this time the 2 mile Kenyon & Leigh Junction Railway had been built to link the Bolton line to the L&M at Kenyon Junction (the world's first main line railway junction between independent companies). This allowed a regular passenger service of two trains each way daily between Bolton's newly built Great Moor Street station and Liverpool to begin on 13th June 1831, taking 100 minutes for the 28½ mile journey, with trains reaching the alarming speed of 35 mph. Passengers from Bolton could also change at Kenyon Junction for Manchester (a north–east link was proposed but never built). The early running of services was let out to private individuals, most notably John Hargreaves of Bolton, who handled the entire working of the line from 1836. This included excursions to Liverpool, Manchester and even London (at a cost of £1 13s 6d for a four-day return in 1843).

In 1845 the Grand Junction Railway took over the line, which became part of the LNWR the following year. Around this time

*Ex-LMS Ivatt class 4MT 2-6-0 no 43026 with a train for Kenyon Junction at Atherton Bag Lane station on the last day of passenger services. (Author's collection)*

loco haulage began on the inclines, and the line lost much of its early importance with the opening of the first direct line between Bolton and Manchester in 1838. By 1852 there were six trains daily each way, with intermediate stations at Daubhill, Chequerbent, Atherton ('Bag Lane' was added in 1924), West Leigh and Bradshaw Leach (renamed Pennington in 1877). In 1858 the loco *Redstart* with 32 wagons ran away down Daubhill incline and demolished the Bolton station. It was patched up and later replaced by a larger station in 1874. Eleven years later, the two inclines were replaced by new double-track lines on easier gradients, with new stations at Chequerbent and Daubhill (now called Rumsworth & Daubhill). Even so the new Chequerbent line was affected by mining subsidence, and eventually became as steep as 1 in 18½ at its lower end – one of the steepest gradients anywhere on British passenger lines.

Regular passenger services continued from Bolton to Liverpool, and until 1942 to Manchester via Tyldesley. The Deansgate

*Bolton's Great Moor Street station shortly before closure in 1954. (Author's collection)*

*A last reminder of the many industrial locos scrapped at Chequerbent – 0-6-0ST 'Robert' rusts away in a corner of the scrapyard. (Author)*

*Kenyon Junction station's Bolton and Leigh platforms in the 1960s, with a Liverpool-bound DMU. (Author's collection)*

branch in Bolton closed in 1930, ending daily delays at level crossings on Crook Street and Great Moor Street, but an additional station was opened at Atherleigh in 1935 to serve nearby housing estates. In 1934 there were twenty weekday departures from Bolton over the line, but by 1953 this was down to six to eight trains to Kenyon Junction and Warrington. The previous year Chequerbent and Rumsworth & Daubhill stations had closed, and the former Bolton & Leigh line's passenger services ended on 27th March 1954, with the 10.35 pm from Great Moor Street to Kenyon Junction hauled by BR-built 2-6-2T no 84003. Rugby League excursions to West Leigh and Wakes Weeks specials from Great Moor Street continued until 1958, when there were nine holiday trains to North Wales on Saturday, 28th June. There was goods traffic into the 1960s, chiefly coal, gravel for motorway construction and water from Burton-upon-Trent for a Bolton brewery! Final closure came in stages from 1963, with the last section – Pennington to Kenyon Junction – closing in 1969.

*By the A6 at Chequerbent, the crossing-keeper's cottage built in 1829 for the original Bolton & Leigh line is still standing though much altered and extended. (Author)*

*The only physical remnant of the former Kenyon & Leigh Junction railway is this bridge at Wilton Lane, which once crossed six lines of track. (Author)*

Nothing remains of the line in Bolton town centre, although some stretches of both lines through Daubhill are identifiable. Remains at Chequerbent are more significant, including stone sleeper blocks from the original incline still visible south of the A6. The 1885 route down from Chequerbent can still be walked (though very muddy in places) to the LYR line of 1888, where the bridge has gone. From there on the route to Kenyon Junction has largely been lost, especially where it has been used for a 4 mile bypass road for Leigh.

# Roe Green Junction to Bolton

This line began and ended its existence as a colliery line, with almost 79 years of passenger services in the middle. The LNWR's 1865 Act was for a line from Roe Green on the Wigan–Eccles line

*A well-tended Walkden Low Level station around 1930. (Stations UK)*

to collieries in the Little Hulton area, south of Bolton, which opened in 1870. The previous year the LNWR had proposed a second Act for the 'Little Hulton Branch Extension' to Bolton's Great Moor Street. This was opposed by the LYR, keen to keep a Manchester–Bolton railway monopoly, but backed by local mine-owners, industrialists and Bolton Corporation, and also the inhabitants of Little Hulton and Walkden who wanted a passenger service. The Act was passed and work began in 1871. Great Moor Street station was rebuilt with a classic 'Italian' style frontage, four waiting rooms and four 300 ft long platforms, and reopened in September 1874, initially for the trains to Leigh. Goods traffic began on the extension later that year, but it was not until 1st April 1875 that passenger trains began from Manchester Victoria, 'with no great ceremony'. Services started with eight weekday trains each way, calling at Plodder Lane, where a four-road (later extended to six) engine shed was also built, Little Hulton and Walkden (Walkden Low Level from 1924) before the junction at Roe Green, where a station was proposed in the 1930s, but never constructed. More significant

*LMS Fowler 2-6-2T no 58 approaches Roe Green Junction with a train for Great Moor Street in June 1947. (W.D. Cooper)*

than the local services were the through carriages for Manchester London Road and London Euston, although these ended during World War I.

As early as the 1930s the need for two lines between Bolton and Manchester was being questioned, and the shorter ex-LYR route via Clifton Junction was always the more likely to be retained. By 1954, services to Roe Green were down to four to five weekday trains each way, and only 360 passengers a day were using Great Moor Street station, for both this line and the trains to Leigh. All its passenger trains ended on 27th March 1954, with the 11 pm departure for Manchester from platform 2. This was worked by Stanier 2-6-4T no 42574 hauling three coaches. Two months later the last 18 engines at Plodder Lane shed were reallocated. Fifty years before there had been twice that number of locos, but with the loss of passenger services it became the first shed in the Manchester area to close. Goods trains continued to use the whole line until 1960, when the section from Roe Green to Little Hulton, which had been the first

*Class 2MT no 84001 about to depart from Plodder Lane station with a Great Moor Street–Manchester Exchange train on the last day of passenger services. (N.R. Knight)*

to open, closed completely. Freight to the Bolton end (via Atherton) lingered for a few more years; Crook Street goods yard closed to BR traffic in 1965 and for the last coal deliveries on 1st October 1967. Great Moor Street station had been knocked down the previous year and the site reused for a leisure pool, but this too was demolished in 2003. Nothing remains at the other station sites, and only traces of the route remain within Bolton. However, south of the M61 almost 3 miles of trackbed, now called the 'Roe Green Loopline', can be walked as far as the former junction.

# Clifton Junction to Bury

This 6 mile stretch was part of the original East Lancashire Railway (ELR) line built northwards to Rawtenstall and opened

*The isolated and little-used station at Ringley Road in the 1920s. (Author's collection)*

*Only the northbound platform and trackbed survive in this wintry scene at Ringley Road. (Author)*

in 1846. Three years later its southernmost end was the scene of a famous railway 'battle'. The ELR was paying to use the LYR line from Clifton into Manchester, but the LYR disputed the payments made. In reprisal, on 12th March 1849 the LYR blocked the line at Clifton, ending up with a total of eight trains, both ELR and LYR ones, stuck at the junction! Although this particular problem was resolved, relations between the two companies continued to be troublesome, until they amalgamated in 1859. Apart from Clifton Junction and Bury Bolton Street, the line opened with only one intermediate station at Radcliffe Bridge. Additional ones were built at quite remote locations at Ringley Road in 1847 and at Molyneux Brow six years later. Two crossings of the Irwell were needed, requiring viaducts near Clifton and at Outwood south of Radcliffe, with in between a lengthy climb at 1 in 96.

Early services included ELR – later LYR – passenger trains to Bury and Bacup, but in 1879 these began running via Prestwich, leaving the Clifton line mostly for trains heading for the ELR extension to Accrington and Colne. These plus services as far as Bury totalled around 25 trains each way on weekdays in 1922. Only eight of these stopped at Ringley Road, and even fewer at Molyneux Brow so it is not surprising that these were early closures, the latter in 1931. Ringley Road lasted until 1953, and Radcliffe Bridge closed five years later, leaving the route with through traffic only. This was only to Accrington in 1964, and as that town's direct route to Manchester had been listed for closure in the Beeching Report, the Clifton–Bury section closed with the ex-ELR lines to Accrington and Bacup on 5th December 1966.

Close to the line's southern end, the thirteen-arch Clifton Viaduct still stands but is closed to public access, while the site of Molyneux Brow station is now beneath the M60 motorway. The northbound platform of Ringley Road station still survives, with seats provided for users of what became a trail for walkers and horse-riders, along almost two miles of the former rail route. The trail was extended in 1999 to the Outwood Viaduct, at one time in a very neglected state despite being a listed structure, but now restored and reopened to the public. Built in 1881 by Andrew Handyside & Co of Derby, its five cast-iron spans are a fine example of Victorian workmanship. Further north, the line

*Outwood Viaduct undergoing complete restoration in 1998. (Author)*

through the site of Radcliffe Bridge station is now a road, while the route into Bury is partly used by the Metrolink tram services from Manchester.

# Bolton–Bury–Rochdale

This line began with an unauthorised 1½ mile link from the Manchester & Leeds Railway at Blue Pitts (Castleton) to Heywood, opened in 1841 and originally worked by horse-drawn trains. It was another seven years before it was extended to Bury and Bolton; by this time the LYR controlled both the line to Leeds and the new extension. The Heywood to Bury section opened on 1st May 1848, and from Bury to Bolton on 20th November. On the same date the LYR opened the line from Bolton to Liverpool via Wigan and Kirkby, thus providing a

*Bradley Fold station in the early years of the 20th century. (J.Ryan collection)*

route to the coast avoiding Manchester, much used by both freight and passenger services.

The station at Heywood was replaced in 1848, and the line's major intermediate station built at Bury. This was initially called Low Level, then Market Place from 1866 to 1888, and finally Knowsley Street. More intermediate stations were built west of Bury at Black Lane, Bradley Fold and Darcy Lever. Connections were provided northwards at Bury onto the former ELR line, and south at Castleton to allow trains to head towards Manchester, and a station was added west of Heywood at Broadfield in 1869. Ten years later a link was put in from Bradley Fold to the LYR's newly opened line from Radcliffe to Manchester via Prestwich, and in 1898 a connection to the Bury–Manchester line, chiefly used for freight heading for Salford Docks. In 1918 the Radcliffe link was used for a railmotor service from Bolton, with an additional halt at Ainsworth Road.

Despite the potential as an east–west through route, the LYR mostly operated local passenger services, with a couple of Blackpool trains. In summer 1922, for example (when the LYR had been taken over by the LNWR), the mainstay of the line was the Bolton–Rochdale passenger service of 22–24 weekday trains. At the western end there were also 14 Bolton–Radcliffe trains, while to the east 17–20 trains ran from Manchester Victoria to Heywood and Bury. Sunday trains on all these routes were in single figures. Trains originating before Bolton peaked under BR; in the 1960s there were through services from Liverpool, Wigan, Southport and Blackpool. The latter of course came into its own at the annual Wakes Weeks; in 1951, for example, 25,000 people left Bury on 50 special trains at the beginning of July. Freight movements too tended to be part of a more regional pattern, with trains from Hull, York and West Yorkshire heading for Liverpool and Salford Docks.

In the Beeching Report the Bolton–Rochdale line was shown as carrying over 50,000 tons of freight a week, and the line was listed for 'modification' rather than closure. Closures had already begun with Darcy Lever station in 1951, and the service to Radcliffe in 1953, although goods and excursion traffic used that line for another eleven years. Despite Beeching,

*Bury Knowsley Street station in 1965, with a Bolton–Rochdale DMU. (B.G. Barlow, courtesy J.A. Peden)*

90

*Stanier 4P no 42647 heading westbound through Heywood station. (C.H.A. Townley, courtesy J.A. Peden)*

the Bolton–Rochdale line was listed for closure in 1964, but reprieved the following year. However, the decline was inexorable; Sunday services ended in September 1964, and through workings from Bacup in 1966. Bury and Heywood goods depots closed in 1967, and the line was again listed for closure the next year. There was fierce local opposition, especially at a public inquiry in June 1969, but by then there were no regular scheduled through passenger workings, and no trains at all after the 8.05 pm from Bolton. In September all intermediate stations, even Bury Knowsley Street, became unstaffed halts. Thus it was probably little surprise that closure was confirmed in May 1970, the last trains running on Saturday 3rd October, with the final departure being the 8.02 pm from Bolton. Six coaches were required, instead of the usual two-car DMU, for the nearly 300 passengers who made this final trip.

The trackbed from Bolton to Radcliffe was retained for a proposed scheme for electric trains into Manchester Victoria.

91

*Darcy Lever Viaduct still towers over the cottages below. (Author)*

*The first day of public services on the reopened Heywood line, 7th September 2003, with restored Black Five no 45157. (J. Suggitt)*

Nothing came of this except the survival of the viaducts at St Peter's Way, Bolton and Darcy Lever, the first iron lattice deck girder bridges in England. Stretches of the trackbed remain, most easily walked east of Bradley Fold station site, and west of Bury where a 'greenway' for walkers and cyclists crosses the five-arch Daisyfield Viaduct. Knowsley Street station was demolished in 1971, but the track east through Heywood has been retained as part of the East Lancashire Railway preserved line. This section was officially reopened on 6th September 2003, using restored Jubilee class 4-6-0 *Leander*, and regular passenger services were running from Bury to Heywood later that year.

# 8
# The LYR Around Oldham

### Werneth, Central and Mumps
### Middleton
### Royton

*Class 8F 2-8-0 no 48329 brings a Blackpool–Failsworth relief train through Royton Junction, with a Royton train at the left and extensive sidings to the right. (J. Davenport)*

## Werneth, Central and Mumps

The Manchester & Leeds Railway (MLR) was built by George Stephenson and was the first line to cross the Pennines. It was being discussed as early as 1825, but it was 1836 before its Act received the royal assent and the first section, between Manchester Oldham Road and Littleborough, opened on 4th July

1839. Its route west into Manchester included Rochdale, although the station was well away from the town centre, but by keeping to the lower ground it bypassed several other growing industrial towns. By far the most important of these was Oldham, with 32,000 inhabitants by 1831, and this was acknowledged by the MLR, which obtained an Act for a branch to the town in 1839. This replaced the original station for Oldham, Mills Hill, with one at Oldham Junction (soon renamed Middleton, and then Middleton Junction in 1852).

*Stanier 4P no 42444 exits from Werneth tunnel into the station. (J. Peden collection)*

*The fine ironwork supporting the canopies is well shown in this early view of Oldham's Central station (Author's collection)*

From the junction, the 1¾ mile branch climbed 182 ft to a new Oldham station at Werneth, a mile west of Oldham town centre. Stephenson believed steam locomotives would not be able to tackle this ascent and so concentrated the climb into ¾ mile at 1 in 27. This was worked by a rope passed round a 17 ft pulley at the top, coaches or wagons on one track being hauled up or lowered down by a balance load of coal or sand on the other track. Despite this primitive arrangement, trainloads of as many as 1,200 passengers were recorded after the opening of the branch in 1842, with ten trains to and from Manchester on weekdays (four or five on Sundays).

Five years later, the branch was extended through tunnels to new stations more conveniently sited for the town, called Central and Mumps (the original becoming Werneth). Thomas Normington was appointed stationmaster of Mumps and wrote his version of the first time a passenger train ascended the incline unaided, possibly in 1849. The rope broke halfway up the incline and the train came to a standstill. The driver was adamant that his engine, with five coaches and a brake van, could not climb

96

the gradient, but was persuaded by Normington to give it a try and on the second attempt from the foot of the incline, the train arrived safely at Werneth. Following this, the LYR (the successor company to the MLR) conducted trials and from the early 1850s the branch became one of the steepest in the country worked by steam traction.

In 1880, the LYR opened a direct line from Thorpes Bridge Junction to Werneth, avoiding the incline. However, it stayed in use for some scheduled passenger trains until 1958, and two years later saw diverted traffic on Sundays in May while the direct line was being re-ballasted. Railtours continued to visit the branch, the last one on 5th January 1963, two days before the line finally closed to freight trains. Stanier 2-8-0 no 48546 attempted the incline with seven brake vans of enthusiasts, only to halt on the icy rails 100 yards from Werneth station. It was an hour

*Photographed in June 2003, a Wigan-bound DMU is about to swing left on the 'direct line' of 1880, with the former Werneth incline straight ahead in the trees. (Author)*

*Oldham Mumps station with a DMU for Shaw & Crompton in June 2003.*
*(Author)*

before the journey was completed with the help of an Austerity loco at the rear. The line was cut back to a 1914 branch into Chadderton coal yard at the foot of the climb. The tracks were lifted in 1964 and the incline has been landscaped, while the siding to the coal yard was lifted later, leaving a clearer footpath along its former trackbed.

Services on the new line to Werneth and Mumps were scheduled to end in 2004, for the line's conversion to another section of Manchester's Metrolink light rail network. Central station had closed long before in 1966; apparently it was thought unnecessary for a town of Oldham's size to keep three stations (out of five built). Now with the Metrolink scheme, the town will have none of its conventional railway stations left, as the route will go through its centre, abandoning the line through Werneth and Mumps.

98

# Middleton

Like Oldham, Middleton was originally served by Mills Hill station on the MLR line of 1839. This was replaced by the station eventually called Middleton Junction in 1842. The following year the MLR sought to build a line to Bury via Middleton, but nothing came of the scheme or an 1846 Act for a line to the town. Eventually, after more failed schemes, the LYR obtained an Act in 1854 and a branch was built, opening on 1st May 1857 with a 6.15 am departure for Manchester and nine trains per day each way in the first timetable. The station, originally with one short platform, was extended to two covered platforms and a range of buildings by 1886, with its last major addition a cotton warehouse in 1908.

Soon there were nineteen weekday trains each way, most going through to Manchester Victoria, and eight on Sundays. Excursion traffic was popular, with 23 trips organised for 1895

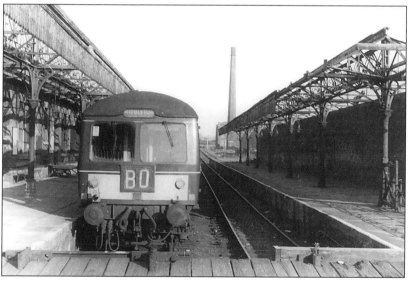

*A deserted and almost derelict Middleton station before closure in 1964. (G. Harrop)*

(not including Wakes Week). Sunday passenger trains ended in 1917, originally as a wartime economy measure, but the usual weekday services continued until the 1940s. Decline then set in with the service down to only six departures a day by the 1960s, and complete closure to passengers on Monday, 7th September 1964, the last train being the 4.49 pm departure on the previous Saturday. Goods traffic lasted until October the following year and Middleton Junction closed in January 1966, leaving the town, now much expanded by Manchester overspill, with no rail access at all.

# Royton

At 1⅜ mile, the shortest line covered in this book, the Royton branch was, like the Middleton branch, built to serve a small cotton-manufacturing town missed out by the MLR in 1839. In this case, access was instead from the 1863 LYR extension north from Oldham Mumps to Rochdale. The branch opened the next year, on 21st March. The small station was provided with a lengthy platform, sufficient for an eight-coach train, and its services were surprisingly frequent as it was effectively the terminus for many of the Manchester Victoria–Oldham trains. In 1922 there were eighteen such arrivals each weekday at Royton, with about the same number going instead to Rochdale. There were another five trains from Oldham Mumps only and one from Middleton Junction. On Sundays there were just six arrivals, all from Manchester. The branch was included in a LMS scheme in 1924 for electrification of the line through Oldham, but nothing came of it.

Even in 1958 there were fifteen to seventeen weekday departures (no Sunday trains by then) but the service was unlikely to survive Beeching. Despite the introduction of two-car DMU sets in the early 1960s, which had increased passenger numbers once more, the branch was scheduled for closure in 1966. The goods trains had already gone two years previously, and the last DMU left at 6.50 pm on 16th April, watched by a crowd of locals despite a heavy downpour. The station at the

*The 'Old Manchester' railtour at Royton station in 1956, with ex-LYR Class
3F 0-6-0 no 52438. This trip was later described as a 'bizarre trainload of
intense antiquarians'! (Author's collection)*

start of the branch, Royton Junction, stayed open until 1987. It
had already been replaced by a new station at Derker, 600 yards
to the south, which will be retained for the Metrolink services to
Rochdale.

# 9
# The 'Delph Donkey'

*Oldham to Greenfield and Delph*

*Oldham Clegg Street station with BR class 2MT no 84015 on the last day of passenger service to Delph. (HMRS/B. Hilton)*

The 'Delph Donkey' was the name given to the passenger service to the Pennine village of Delph right up to closure in 1955. There has long been argument over whether this originated from an early service using a horse-drawn coach, but this has never been confirmed. The villages around Delph were all within the West Riding of Yorkshire up to 1974, when they were included within Greater Manchester, and are now part of the borough of Oldham. The first railway in the vicinity was the Huddersfield &

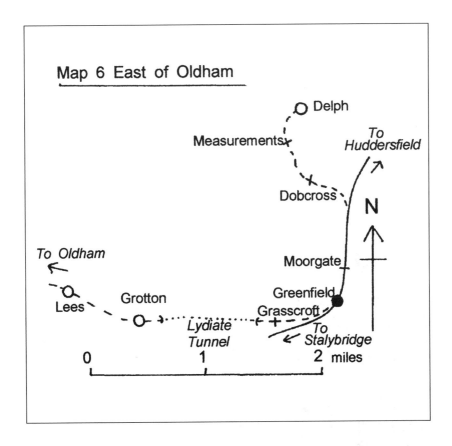

Map 6 East of Oldham

Manchester, part of the LNWR by the time it opened in 1849. Its Act had included powers for a branch to Delph, and a 1½ mile single-track branch from Greenfield on the main line opened on 1st September 1851. The terminus was at New Delph, ½ mile from the village, where its largest textile mills (producing woollen cloth rather than cotton) had been built. Initially there were four return journeys on weekdays only, and no intermediate stations on the branch. Five years later, Greenfield was linked to Oldham (that town's second railway) and the service became Delph–Oldham, though soon reduced to only two trains a day! At first these ran to a temporary LNWR station by the LYR Mumps station, but in 1862 the LNWR extended the line to

*Lees engine shed seen before closure in 1964, with at the right Fairburn class 4P no 42115. (J. Davenport)*

Oldham's Clegg Street station and replaced the temporary one at Mumps with Glodwick Road station. The line's main feature was the 1,332 yards long Lydiate tunnel built on a 1 in 100 gradient up from Greenfield. At its western end was Grotton station, followed by another intermediate station at Lees, where an engine shed was added in 1878.

Delph's passenger service gradually improved to five daily trains in 1879, and eleven in 1910. A further increase came with the introduction of 'push and pull' services in 1912. There were now thirteen trains each weekday and three new halts were opened. These were at Grasscroft, on the line to Oldham west of Greenfield, at Moorgate on the Stalybridge–Huddersfield main line (but served only by Delph trains), and at Dobcross on the branch itself. Another halt on the branch was added in 1932 to serve the nearby Measurements Mill, and the following year saw the peak for passenger services on the line, with 22 Greenfield–Delph weekday trains, most of them from Oldham Clegg Street.

*Ex-LMS Fowler 2-6-2T no 40056 with a Delph-bound train at Measurements halt, with the mill just visible at the left. (J. Davenport)*

*The rear trailer coach of a push-pull train at Delph station, shortly before closure of the branch. (J. Davenport)*

*The former station building at Delph is still in use as a private residence. (Author)*

As well as the scheduled services, excursion traffic had long been important. There were trains to take local people out of the area, especially on 19th century Wakes Week trips to Blackpool and Belle Vue pleasure gardens in Manchester, and trains into this scenic corner of the Pennines. In 1875, for example, 300 members of the Temperance Union travelled to Delph by train, while in 1898 a trip was organised for 800 Oldham school-children. Freight was also significant; movements of coal, stone and textiles were important, but the line's peak came in the late 1880s with the construction of the Castleshaw reservoirs. This involved temporarily extending the line past Delph station for the contractor's traffic, with several work trains a day.

From the 1920s, increased competition from road traffic began to affect the branch. Excursion traffic did not survive the Second World War, and the scheduled service dwindled from nineteen daily trains in 1937 to fourteen in 1954, although the summers of 1953 and 1954 saw the first ever Sunday trains – nine Oldham–

*The former Grotton station building was rapidly being hidden by trees in 1997, although a platform and the trackbed leading to Lydiate tunnel remain clear. (Author)*

Delph return trains. But in March 1955 BR applied to close the line, claiming losses of £28,000 a year, and on Saturday, 30th April the final passenger trains ran. Last of all was the 11.10 pm from Clegg Street to Delph, with 600 rather than the usual 60 passengers, which then had to return them to Oldham instead of running back empty. Freight lasted another eight years, by then down to a weekly coal shipment rather than a daily goods train. Passenger services from Oldham to Greenfield had also finished in 1955, including Glodwick Road station, the first of Oldham's five stations to close. The last freight working through Lydiate tunnel was on 10th April 1964; two days later the line finally closed, along with Lees engine shed.

Later in 1964, the track was lifted; by then there was little sign of the halts, although the stationmaster's house at Grotton and station building at Delph still survive as residences. Most of the Delph branch can be walked, as can the route into Oldham from the Grotton station site. This has been landscaped as a 'linear park' through Lees, where nothing remains of the station or engine shed, and on towards the site of Glodwick Road station. Beyond this, most of the route through to Clegg Street has been lost to redevelopment.

107

# 10
# Around Guide Bridge and Stalybridge

*Oldham–Ashton–Guide Bridge*
*Denton to Ashton, Droylsden and Stalybridge*
*The Micklehurst Loop*

*Class 2MT no 84013 at Oldham Clegg Street with the 6.04 pm from Stockport Edgeley via the OA&GB in April 1959. The adjacent Central station is at the right. (HMRS/B. Hilton)*

## Oldham–Ashton–Guide Bridge

In the 19th century, Ashton-under-Lyne was one of the towns east of Manchester that were growing rapidly with the

*Fairburn 4P no 42114 on a Huddersfield–Stockport train at Park Bridge station in late summer 1954. (J. Davenport)*

expanding cotton industry. It features in the title of the Sheffield, Ashton-under-Lyne & Manchester Railway (MS&L from 1847), which opened its first line from Manchester to Godley in 1841. This included a station called Ashton, but this was two miles from the town and four years later was renamed Guide Bridge. Within ten years, it had become a major junction, with the line to Godley extended to Sheffield, and new lines to Stalybridge and Stockport. One omission was any link to Oldham, despite attempts by groups within that town to get such a line built. It was left to the MS&L and LNWR to jointly propose the Oldham, Ashton & Guide Bridge Junction Railway (OA&GB) in 1857, to run from the LNWR's temporary station at Oldham Mumps to the LYR west of Ashton and then on to Guide Bridge.

Construction was delayed on the Oldham–Ashton section by the need for a viaduct at Park Bridge with a major embankment south of it, and two short tunnels. Eventually the line opened on 31st July 1861, with a special train from Manchester London

*A train from Guide Bridge heads for Oldham in October 1958, headed by ex-GCR Robinson class C13 4-4-2T no 67414, which seven months later headed the last such train. (HMRS/B. Hilton)*

Road, consisting of thirteen carriages for about 200 'gentlemen', whose journey was accompanied by a band from the 3rd Regiment of the Manchester Volunteers. Public services began a month later, with seven weekday MS&L trains from London Road (five on Sundays). There was no connection with the LYR east into Ashton, and so a separate Ashton station (later called Ashton Oldham Road) was built together with other intermediate stations at Park Bridge and Ryecroft on Ashton Moss (which only lasted eighteen months). A new station was provided at Oldham, Clegg Street, which after rebuilding in 1900 became the largest of the town's five stations, with a 270 ft long main platform and a refreshment room!

The LNWR joined in providing passenger trains from 1869, including a through service from Rochdale to London Euston (there was already a similar service to London King's Cross). There were also trains from Oldham to Stalybridge, Stockport (see next section), Marple, Glossop and Macclesfield, and

110

*Black Five no 45340 passing OA&GB East Junction with a Manchester–Leeds semi-fast train around 1960. (Author's collection)*

through Oldham from Guide Bridge to Delph. By 1922 two local services were the main users of the line – the LNWR Manchester London Road service via Guide Bridge, and GCR trains from Stockport to Oldham, some continuing to Rochdale. Both provided eleven weekday trains (three to five on Sundays), but competition from trams, trolleybuses and later buses was intense. As early as 1928 Manchester and Oldham were linked by an express bus service, and with increasing private car ownership trains between the local industrial towns were doomed. The long-distance trains were the first to go, the London service was down to a single through carriage for Oldham and Rochdale by the 1930s, while the local passenger trains survived until 2nd May 1959. Clegg Street station appeared to have a future as the parcels depot for the whole Oldham area, and Park Bridge Viaduct was rebuilt in 1960, but the parcels traffic ended in 1967 and Clegg Street station and the Oldham–Ashton section closed. South from Oldham, the route can be walked to within ½ mile of the former OA&GB East Junction at Ashton, with a detour at

Park Bridge where the viaduct was demolished in 1971. The line south from Ashton remains in use for freight, although the curve to Guide Bridge station has now been lifted. Both these sections are part of the Central Railway's proposals for a route from the Channel Tunnel to Seaforth Docks at Liverpool.

# Denton to Ashton, Droylsden and Stalybridge

By the late 19th century, Guide Bridge was becoming a serious bottleneck for the railways east of Manchester. To ease the congestion, the LNWR built a series of avoiding lines from Denton Junction on its 1849 Stockport–Guide Bridge line. The first of these was a 1¼ mile loop west of Guide Bridge to Crowthorn Junction on the OA&GB, opened in 1876. This

*The Denton Junction–Crowthorn Junction line is still in use for freight; here class 47 no 47003 heads towards Denton in 1988. (J.A.G.H. Coltas)*

112

*A Manchester–Mossley train with Stanier 4P no 42551 at Droylsden station; the Denton line branched off behind the building on the left. (J. Davenport)*

allowed freight to bypass Guide Bridge from 14th February, while two months later a Stockport–Ashton–Oldham passenger service began. In 1925 there were fourteen trains each way on weekdays (five on Sundays) using this route between Stockport and Oldham, but by 1951 the pressure on Guide Bridge had eased enough for the cut-off to be abandoned, and the service finished altogether with the closure of the former OA&GB line to passengers in 1959. However, this is the only one of the routes dealt with here still in use for freight.

In 1882, the LNWR built a line north from this first cut-off at Ashton Moss Junction to Droylsden station, opened in 1846 on the main line from Manchester Victoria to Huddersfield and Leeds. This allowed access for freight to the yards at Miles Platting, and for passenger trains from Euston, Crewe and Stockport to Manchester Victoria. It was particularly useful for the London service for East Lancashire, which began in 1905; this usually consisted of through carriages for Colne detached at Stockport and sent on via Droylsden. In 1955 two such trains

113

*Despite closure in 1905, the original Audenshaw station building still stands, with 'Station House' to the right. (Author)*

remained, with a third involving a change at Stockport. Around 1960 the line saw much passenger traffic from London Euston diverted to Victoria while London Road was reconstructed as Piccadilly. The same happened in the early 1970s, this time while the West Coast Main Line was being electrified, but this was the last use of the line; passenger trains to Colne using this route had ended in 1962, and Droylsden station closed six years later. Much earlier there had also been Stockport–Manchester trains, though by 1922 only one train a day was calling at Droylsden on this service and the other intermediate station at Audenshaw had closed as early as 1905. The route can be walked between those two station sites, though much of it has been landscaped.

The third avoiding route ran to the east of Guide Bridge, from Denton Junction to Stalybridge, and was completed in 1893. It provided for a Stockport–Stalybridge passenger service, calling at Dukinfield & Ashton and Hooley Hill. The LNWR used the latter as an alternative station to Guide Bridge, but it was closed between 1917 and 1921 and renamed Audenshaw in 1924. Two years previously there had been a weekday service of eleven trains each way but no Sunday service. On 25th September 1950 the local passenger trains ended, and the line was lifted some twenty years later. Now it is difficult to see any remnants of the route at all.

# The Micklehurst Loop

Guide Bridge station was not the only source of congestion for the LNWR in the late 19th century. Its main line from Liverpool and Manchester across the Pennines to Huddersfield and Leeds depended on Standedge, the longest tunnel in England when

*Stanier 8F no 48252 hauls a freight train on the Micklehurst Loop in the 1960s. (J. Davenport)*

115

*The short-lived Micklehurst station building in 1998; the main building shown was the stationmaster's residence, with at the right the single-storey former booking office. (Author)*

opened in 1849, but only single track. A second single-track tunnel (1871) was still insufficient, so in 1894 a third tunnel, this time double-track, was opened, finally providing four tracks. However, this was achieved between Stalybridge and the tunnel not by quadrupling the track through Greenfield, but by the construction of a completely separate double-track line on the other side of the Tame valley – the Micklehurst Loop.

The loop opened nine years before the third tunnel, on 1st December 1885, and was primarily for diversions and freight, particularly eastbound goods trains, as the uphill gradients were easier than on the earlier line. However, in the following year the LNWR reluctantly began local passenger services to stations at Slaley & Millbrook, Micklehurst, Friezland and Uppermill. The first two of these closed by the end of 1909, but the others lasted until 1st January 1917, when they were closed as a wartime economy measure but never reopened despite the efforts of the local councils.

The line continued busy with freight right up to the 1950s; in 1952, for example, as many as 32 eastbound goods trains alone were recorded on a typical weekday. In spite of this, the general rundown of the railways soon meant that four tracks were no longer needed for the Tame valley and Standedge tunnels. The line closed to regular freight traffic on 7th September 1964 and for diversions two years later, when the old single-track Standedge tunnels were also shut. A single track was left at the southern end of the loop to serve the power station near Millbrook until 1976. The previous year the line's sixteen-arch blue brick viaduct east of Greenfield was demolished to make way for a £165,000 'linear park'; thus much of the route is still walkable, though heavily landscaped in places.

# 11
# Manchester's Closed Termini

*Liverpool Road station*
*Exchange station*
*Central station*

*Where it all began – restoration since this 1974 view of Liverpool Road station has largely kept the 19th century frontage intact. (Author's collection)*

## Liverpool Road station

Liverpool Road station is probably the railways' most significant site in NW England, and its booking halls and waiting rooms can claim to be the oldest passenger station in the world to be served by locomotive-hauled trains. Yet the station building is only the centrepiece of a complex that includes the world's oldest railway warehouse and three other 19th century railway buildings, on a site not originally chosen for a railway terminus at all. The Liverpool & Manchester Railway Act of 1826 was the first for a railway intended to carry passengers (earlier lines such as the Stockton & Darlington Railway of 1825 were primarily for goods). The Act specified a site for the Manchester terminus on the south side of the New Bailey prison, by the river Irwell. However, another Act three years later changed this to one in Liverpool Road, more convenient for the Rochdale and Bridgewater Canals.

As built, the station comprised a single platform with two booking offices and waiting rooms, and a separate warehouse, where the banquet for the Duke of Wellington and other dignitaries was held at the line's opening ceremony on 15th September 1830, with public traffic commencing two days later. The world's first carriage of the mail by train began in November that year, and by 1831 as many as 2,000 to 2,500 passengers were using the line every day. In May that year goods services began, and it was these that kept the station in use for well over a century when passenger services ended in 1844.

The opening of the MLR's final section in 1841 completed the east–west link between Hull and Liverpool, apart from a gap between Liverpool Road station and the MLR terminus on Oldham Road. This was solved by the construction of a station at Hunts Bank, to be called Victoria. When the rail links to that station were completed in 1844, Liverpool Road closed to passengers and was relegated to goods duties, which continued until closure on 8th September 1975. The station remained disused until 1978, when British Rail offered it to Greater Manchester Council for the token price of £1, along with £100,000 towards restoration. Basic repairs were done to allow public access to the site for the 150th anniversary of the Liverpool & Manchester Railway in 1980, but comprehensive restoration was needed before the buildings could house Manchester's Museum of Science and Industry, transferred there in 1983.

Now the former 1st class booking hall has a representation of how it might have looked in the 1830s, and there are displays in

*Behind the frontage Liverpool Road was still a working goods yard in 1974. (Author's collection)*

*The same scene today, looking very different after restoration as the Manchester Museum of Science and Industry. (Author)*

*The recreation of the 1830 1st class booking hall is part of the museum's displays at Liverpool Road station. (Author)*

the waiting room and the 2nd class booking hall. These continue into the rebuilt shops and offices of 1830/1, with the former carriage shed now used in part for the museum's Design Studio. Elsewhere on the site can be seen part of the brick viaduct with its twenty-three arches that carried the original line a further 200 metres from the crossing of the Irwell, while the 1830 warehouse has further displays. Yet more 19th century railway buildings are used for the museum's Main Building and for its display of engines, with examples of locomotives built in Greater Manchester, including the largest ever built in Europe. This is certainly a museum with plenty for the railway enthusiast.

# Exchange station

Exchange is very much the poor relation of Manchester's closed city centre station sites, particularly as, unlike the other two,

*Exchange's trainshed is shown to good effect with a BR equivalent of the Black Five, Standard class 5 no 73096. (G. Harrop)*

almost nothing survives. Often regarded merely as an adjunct of nearby Victoria, it was in fact built as a separate station. As Victoria's traffic expanded during the 19th century, it became impossible to accommodate all its services despite expansion to a total of seventeen platforms by 1904. In addition the LYR, which had built Victoria in 1844, refused to let the LNWR share ownership. Thus in June 1884, the LNWR opened its own Exchange station, named after the nearby Cotton Exchange and in Salford rather than Manchester. This meant a walk of ¼ mile for passengers between the two stations through the older part of Victoria. The new station's three through platforms and two bays handled the LNWR's services to North Wales, Liverpool and Leeds, leaving Victoria to concentrate on serving industrial Lancashire and Yorkshire.

In 1929 the LMS combined Exchange's platform 3 with Victoria's platform 11 to make a single platform of 2,235 ft – the longest in Europe. Exchange suffered serious bomb damage during air raids in 1940; the refreshment room and the Italianate

*In March 1966, Black Five no 45279 is about to leave for one of Exchange's main destinations – the North Wales coast. (Author's collection)*

frontage were demolished and never rebuilt – the station was merely patched up. In the early 1960s Exchange was still dealing with 60 arrivals and 60 departures a day, including the successors to the famous Club trains. These were first set up by the LYR for its Blackpool services in 1895, and consisted of a 'superior' 1st class carriage attached to an express and reserved for the members of an exclusive group of businessmen. The LNWR's equivalents ran from Exchange to Windermere and Llandudno, and were lettered in gold 'Club Carriage for Members Only'! All NW England's Club trains were continued by the LMS in the 1920s and 30s, but did not long survive nationalisation, although the 4.30 pm departure from Exchange for Llandudno was still regarded by businessmen as 'their' train well into the 1960s. However, declining traffic meant there was no longer a need for two adjacent stations, and Exchange closed on 5th May 1969, when all its passenger trains transferred to Victoria. It was demolished in 1981 and the site is now used as a car park.

# Central station

While Liverpool Road station undoubtedly has the historical edge, it is Central station that has the visual impact amongst Manchester's railway remains. Its 210 ft wide single span roof (exceeded in the UK only by London's St Pancras station) rises 90 ft and continues to be a dominant feature of the city skyline. Its railway origins date back to a temporary building erected on an adjacent site by the CLC in 1877. Work had already begun on the present structure, with its magnificent 550 ft long roof constructed by Andrew Handyside & Co of Derby, and this was completed and opened for rail services on 1st July 1880. The building was basically a trainshed over six platforms, with a seventh platform outside and two more added later; offices and waiting rooms were in a 'temporary' wooden structure which was never replaced. The Midland began using the station from

*LNER class D6 no 5855 (built by the MS&L) still in use as the station pilot engine at Manchester's Central station in 1946, a year before it was withdrawn. (Author's collection)*

*Now Central station is an outstanding example of the reuse of station property – converted into the G-Mex Centre. (Author)*

August 1880 and its services to St Pancras were much improved by the opening of the direct line through Disley tunnel in 1902. By this time the GCR and GNR were also using Central as the departure point for London expresses via Guide Bridge to Marylebone and King's Cross respectively, providing effective competition for the LNWR at London Road (later Piccadilly), with a total of over 400 train movements daily.

The GNR services did not survive World War I, and in LNER days most former GCR expresses ran into London Road station instead. By the 1960s the only London services were those using the former Midland line, including the 'Midland Pullman' hauled by diesel-electric locos achieving journey times to St Pancras of 3 hours 13 minutes. However, these ended with the electrification of the line from Piccadilly to Euston, which was completed in 1966, and services from Central went into rapid decline. In January 1967 the 'South District' local trains ended (see Chapter 12) and the stopping service to Chinley and Sheffield transferred

*Across from the former Central station is Manchester's Crowne Plaza Midland Hotel, opened by the Midland Railway in 1903. (Author)*

to Piccadilly. Later the same year, the stopping service to Derby also ended. Most crucially, on 1st January 1968, the expresses to Derby and St Pancras were withdrawn, leaving only the ex-CLC routes to Liverpool and Chester with which the station had started. These only lasted another 17 months and Central and its approaches closed completely on 5th May 1969.

Before British Rail relinquished the site in 1972, the station was given Listed status (Grade 2), which should have ensured its future. This was often in doubt in the decade that followed as the building passed through various ownerships including that of a demolition and scrap recovery company! After complex negotiations, the Greater Manchester Council acquired title to the site. This led to the conversion of the station building for exhibitions and events, and its reopening as the G-Mex Centre on 21st March 1986. Since then it has been in use as an exhibition centre for about 80% of the year, and can also be used as an arena seating 5,500 people or a concert hall for audiences of up to 9,000.

Across the street from the former station is the Crowne Plaza Midland Hotel. Despite the original intention for the three owner companies of the CLC (the GNR, the MS&L and the Midland Railway) to build a combined office block and hotel at the front of the station, it was the Midland Railway that bought a site opposite for £365,000 in 1896. Seven years later, its hotel opened, complete with a covered walkway from the rear to the station, allowing guests to walk to their train (or carriage) protected from the Manchester weather. This no longer exists but the renovated building still stands as a outstanding example of a railway hotel.

# 12
# South Manchester

*The Midland Railway through Didsbury*
*The Fallowfield Loop*

*An example of the South Manchester lines' long-distance traffic is shown here at Wilbraham Road, with a Liverpool–Hull express hauled by ex-LNER class K3/2 2-6-0 no 61852. (Author's collection)*

## The Midland Railway through Didsbury

In 1864 a Manchester & Cheadle Railway was proposed but not built. Nine years later the scheme was revived as the Manchester South District Railway (MSDR), this time to go as far as Alderley. The Midland was at that time using London Road station for its services to St Pancras, and saw the South District scheme as an alternative, which would provide a link to the Central station

*The scene at Didsbury station in Midland Railway days, around 1910.
(J.A. Peden collection)*

being developed by the CLC. Although the MSDR obtained its own Act in 1873, four years later it was vested in the Midland, which built and operated the line. So what began as a proposal for a suburban line through southern Manchester became a Midland main line to London!

The 6 mile line from Throstle Nest East Junction, west of Manchester Central station, to Heaton Mersey Junction west of Stockport opened on 1st January 1880, with intermediate stations at Chorlton-cum-Hardy, Withington, Didsbury and Heaton Mersey. Later that year there were fourteen daily South District local trains to Stockport Tiviot Dale, and twelve long-distance trains for Derby, Nottingham, Leicester and London. The local trains proved popular with residents of the fast-growing suburbs of South Manchester, with over 200,000 passenger bookings in 1900 at both Didsbury and Withington (Withington & Albert Park since 1884). By then the Midland was building its £2 million new line from Heaton Mersey south through new stations at Cheadle Heath and Hazel Grove to Disley tunnel and New Mills. Cheadle Heath opened as an alternative destination for South

129

*Heaton Mersey was the most remote and least-used of the South District stations, but still managed a staff of ten in this scene around 1920. (J.A. Peden collection)*

*By contrast Cheadle Heath was built as a main line station and is seen here with a South District local train headed by Midland 'Flatiron' 0-6-4T no 2008 around 1908. (Author's collection)*

District local trains on 1st October 1901, while Midland expresses were able to use the line from July 1902. From this time, competition from trams began to affect the northern part of the route, and passenger bookings at Withington & Albert Park were down by a third between 1900 and 1910.

Despite increasing competition from road transport, stations such as Didsbury saw over forty passenger trains each way on weekdays up to 1939. Trains ran with an average ten minute frequency at morning and evening peak times, and continued up to an 11.15 pm departure from Central, often referred to as the 'theatre train' as it was much used by local residents returning from performances in Manchester. Interests of a different kind were catered for by two Sunday 'hikers' specials', departing Didsbury at 8.48 and 9.02 am for Chinley and the Peak District. Didsbury was also a stop for two London weekday morning expresses, reaching the capital in four hours, and for their equivalent evening return trains.

After World War II the local service went into decline; in 1950, for example, the usage from Withington (by then Withington & West Didsbury) was put at only 30 regular daily passengers. In the 1950s the typical stock was reduced from seven to four carriages, and in 1956 the local service was down to sixteen daily trains. However, the long-distance trains became more important between 1958 and 1966 when the line handled the bulk of the Manchester–London services while the route via Crewe was being electrified, with Cheadle Heath the only call for the otherwise non-stop 'Midland Pullman'. Despite the introduction of DMUs early in 1961, the local service was past saving. Later that year, on 3rd July, Heaton Mersey and Withington & West Didsbury closed. The remaining stations struggled on until 2nd January 1967, when the local passenger services to both Cheadle Heath and Stockport Tiviot Dale were withdrawn. Two years later Central station closed and the line shut completely in 1970.

The line through Cheadle Heath still has a single track, though for freight only. Elsewhere most of the route has remained intact, but the stations were all demolished, although Withington's platforms survive. A stretch of almost a mile between the station sites at Didsbury and Heaton Mersey is walkable as the 'Midland Railway Path'. The route as far as East Didsbury was one of six

*The line through Cheadle Heath is still in use for freight, although this scene with 8F no 8703 is from 1948. (Author's collection)*

originally chosen in the 1980s for Manchester's Metrolink light railway system (and the only one based on a disused railway). However, progress on this route has been slow. While others have been built and opened as phases 1 and 2, the proposed line through Didsbury to Stockport was left to phase 3, and even then not as one of three core routes intended for completion by 2010. One of these will be the line to Manchester Airport, which will use 1¾ miles of the former line through Chorlton-cum-Hardy, where the station site is to be used as a 'stop'. In 2003 the rest of the line was still awaiting a public inquiry on the route between East Didsbury and Stockport, and possible 'further government support', so walkers should have the 'Midland Railway Path' for some time!

# The Fallowfield Loop

The name and location suggest a suburban route through southern Manchester, but this line was part of major cross-

*A local service from Guide Bridge to Manchester Central at Wilbraham Road in 1948 (its 0-6-2T loco had been built by the MS&L in the 1890s). (J.D. Darby)*

country routes and at one stage looked to have a long-term future after electrification. The 7 mile double-track line was built by the Manchester, Sheffield & Lincolnshire Railway (MS&L) at a cost of £138,880, and was completed in 1892. It linked the Manchester South District line at Chorlton Junction to the MS&L main line at Fairfield, where a new station with six platforms replaced the earlier one ¼ mile to the west. Intermediate stations were provided at Alexandra Park (Wilbraham Road from 1923), Fallowfield, Levenshulme (which added 'South' in 1952) and Hyde Road. The Great Central (the name taken by the MS&L in 1897) ran the line's local services, with twenty to twenty-one weekday stopping trains from Manchester Central to Guide Bridge in 1903, and seven on Sundays.

By the 1930s, the LNER had reduced the local service to seven trains each way, with an extra Saturday lunchtime train, but no Sunday service. However, the line was used by a similar number of long-distance passenger trains. These included the

*The Liverpool–Harwich Boat Train headed by Stanier 4P no 42628 comes off the Fallowfield Loop at Fairfield in April 1961. (T. Lewis, courtesy J.A. Peden)*

Liverpool–Harwich Boat Trains, considered the highlight of the day by local enthusiasts, and the 3.20 pm departure from London Marylebone, also regarded as a 'star turn'. Other long-distance trains ran to Sheffield and Leicester, and there was a regular Liverpool Central–Hull service. This, like the Boat Trains, continued into the 1960s, despite the need for reversing at Manchester Central. After the 1954 electrification of the Woodhead tunnel route, a loco change was also needed at Guide Bridge. The easternmost two miles of the line were electrified for an electric train depot at Reddish, and phase 4 of the scheme would have seen this extended over the whole line to Central, but it never happened. By 1958, local services were down to three or four Manchester–Guide Bridge trains on weekdays only, and these were withdrawn on 7th July 1958, when the stations, still with gas lamps named for each place, closed to passengers.

The through passenger services ended with the closure of Manchester Central in 1969, but long-distance freight trains

*Fallowfield station building survives and is shown here in use as a bar in 2001. (Author)*

continued on the line for another 20 years, though it was singled in the 1970s and the last regular use was in October 1988. After this the route lay abandoned until Sustrans began converting it for use as a cycleway in 2001. Two years later, a new Fallowfield Loop was opened as the first stage of the Manchester Cycleway, Britain's longest off-road urban route for cyclists. It can also be used by walkers and the first four miles have a bridleway for horse riders. Little remains of the former railway although the station building at Fallowfield still stands.

# 13
# The CLC Through Stockport

*Glazebrook to Skelton Junction*
*Skelton Junction to Stockport*
*Stockport to Woodley, Romiley and Reddish*
*Woodley to Godley*

*Ex-LMS Fowler class 4F 0-6-0 no 44456 heads through Stockport Tiviot Dale station en route for Heaton Mersey shed in November 1964. (G. Harrop)*

## Glazebrook to Skelton Junction

Another railway once branched off south-east at Glazebrook, still an operational station on the former Cheshire Lines Committee (CLC) Liverpool–Manchester line. This formed the westernmost

*Ex-Midland class 4F 0-6-0 no 43843 descends the embankment from the crossing of the Manchester Ship Canal in May 1957. (J.A. Peden)*

part of the CLC's through route via Stockport to Godley on the Woodhead line into Yorkshire. The Glazebrook–Skelton Junction section was opened in 1873, with intermediate stations at Cadishead, Partington and West Timperley. By 1887 there were seventeen weekday trains each way, linking Liverpool Central and Warrington with Stockport, Hull, Bristol and London St Pancras.

In 1893 the line achieved the unusual distinction of being largely reopened on a different alignment. The construction of the Manchester Ship Canal required railway viaducts high enough for ocean-going ships to pass beneath. The solution for the Glazebrook–Skelton Junction section was a parallel line climbing to cross the canal, then descending to Partington Junction. This required new stations for Cadishead and Partington, which opened to passengers on 29th May 1893. East of the canal the old line was transferred to the canal company, which used it for access to a coaling basin up to 1966.

The line was never important for local services; for example,

137

*The abandoned and sealed-off viaduct at Cadishead still towers 75 ft above the Manchester Ship Canal. (Author)*

eastbound in 1922 there were only five stopping weekday trains, and no Sunday service. Instead long-distance traffic, both freight and passenger trains, kept the line busy, particularly after the opening in 1902 of the 'Liverpool Curve' at Cheadle Heath, which gave the Midland access to the route. It was the closure of Liverpool Central (except for the Gateacre service) in 1966 that ended passenger traffic over the line. Local trains had already ended on 30th November 1964, but freight continued to be important. Even here decline set in during the next 20 years, with the end of coal shipments, the closures of both Irlam steel works and Carrington power station, and the rundown of the once-massive Shell chemical works. The line was singled in 1984, and eventually the only trains were those bringing polypropylene to the chemical plant; the last of these ran on 10th October 1993 and the following year the line was closed. It remains in track from Skelton Junction to Partington, but the line over the canal has been lifted, leaving only the viaduct.

# Skelton Junction to Stockport

This line was built by one of the four original companies that formed the CLC, the Stockport, Timperley & Altrincham Junction Railway (ST&AJ), although that company's line extended to Deansgate Junction outside Altrincham in the west and to a station at Portwood, east of Stockport. It opened on 1st December 1865 with a new Stockport station at Tiviot Dale (originally Teviot Dale), and the following year intermediate stations at Cheadle (Cheadle North from 1950), Northenden and Baguley were added. The line was already linked at its eastern end to the MS&L at Woodley, and further links were made in 1866, both west to Broadheath Junction (for Lymm and Warrington) and east to Godley for the Woodhead line. The final CLC link was the line north-west to Glazebrook, allowing a Stockport to Liverpool Brunswick service to begin in 1873.

*Baguley station was built to a standard design for CLC stations. (The platform at the extreme right was used for a famed local passenger service – the 'Baguley Bus' – up to 1931.) (G. Harrop)*

139

*The CLC never owned its own locomotives, but did run Sentinel steam railcars in the 1930s. Here no 600 is seen at Cheadle station. (Lens of Sutton Association)*

However, other companies put in yet more links. The MS&L added an east–north curve at Skelton Junction for a short-lived 'circular' service between London Road and Central stations via Stockport (1879–80). The LNWR opened a branch from Northenden Junction to Stockport, with its own Cheadle station, and a regular passenger service from there to London Road ran until the LNWR Cheadle station closed in 1917. Finally the Midland gained access to the line with its 'Liverpool Curve' at Cheadle Heath in 1902.

With all these connections, it is hardly surprising that this became one of the busiest freight lines in the country. Even as late as the 1950s over 250 trains daily passed through Skelton Junction, excluding local passenger traffic which by then was in decline. It ended completely on 30th November 1964, with the closure of Cheadle North, Northenden and Baguley stations. Stockport Tiviot Dale lasted a little longer, shutting with the end of the South District services in 1967. Five years earlier, typical

140

weekday eastbound passenger trains included ten to Sheffield or Derby and one through to St Pancras, as well as numerous South District arrivals, and five trains from Warrington or Liverpool via Skelton Junction. All these were ended by the run-down of services at Manchester's and Liverpool's Central stations.

Reputedly built for £8,000, Tiviot Dale station received favourable comments for its exterior, described in 1879 as a 'pretty brick building' with its arcaded frontage of 30 bays. The approval did not extend to its interior, variously described as 'forever grimy', 'almost permanently gloomy' and 'dark, dank and foreboding'. By mid-1967 it had been demolished, but freight movements continued up to 1980 when damage caused by the construction of the M63 (now M60) motorway led to the suspension of services. Two years later the closure was made permanent.

Freight does still continue, using the 'Liverpool Curve' and the original ST&AJ curve towards Altrincham at Skelton Junction. In

*The unmistakable CLC-designed former Cheadle station building has been preserved as the 'Cheshire Line Tavern'. (Author)*

141

2003 around twenty trains a week used this route each way for
movements of limestone, steel, cement and coal. More surprising
has been the return of passenger trains to the line's western half.
Since 1988 trains have joined the line from the former LNWR
branch at Northenden Junction and covered four miles of the
original ST&AJ route past the sites of Northenden and Baguley
stations to Deansgate Junction. This has restored a regular
service between Stockport and Altrincham, previously withdrawn
in 1931!

# Stockport to Woodley, Romiley and Reddish

The CLC route through Stockport continued over the rest of the
ex-ST&AJ line to Portwood, which was replaced as a passenger
station by Tiviot Dale and relegated to goods duties in 1875.

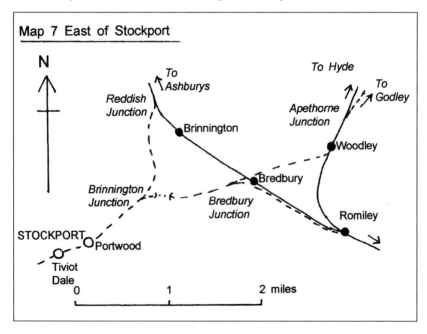

*Woodley station dates back to the 1860s, when the facilities included a refreshment room! The former line to Stockport can be seen heading right beyond the now disused building. (Author)*

Heading east, the line was formerly the Stockport & Woodley Junction Railway, one of the original CLC companies, linking the town to the MS&L and opened in 1863. Woodley station had already opened the previous year, on the MS&L extension from its Hyde branch to Marple. There were no intermediate stations on the Stockport–Woodley line and the main feature was the steep climb eastwards, often requiring the use of a banking engine for freight trains. Two tunnels were needed at Brinnington; the shorter western one was opened out in 1931 when the last section was demolished at 6 am on Sunday, 12th January in time for the 9.02 am 'hikers' special' departure from Tiviot Dale for Chinley and the Hope Valley! Such passenger trains ended in 1967, but through freight heading for the Woodhead line continued until the closure of the line through Stockport in 1980. This severed the line's westward connections, and it was

143

*Stanier 8F no 48161 exits from the surviving Brinnington tunnel with a freight train for Godley in June 1962. (J.A.G.H. Coltas)*

further shortened by the extension of the M63 across its route. However, a length of track still remains at the Woodley end to serve industrial premises. Nearer to Stockport, almost a mile of the route can be walked, including the surviving Brinnington tunnel.

The western section of the Stockport–Woodley line gained more traffic in 1875, when a link was opened from Bredbury Junction to Romiley. This gave the Midland access through Tiviot Dale, first for its St Pancras–Liverpool trains, followed by those to Manchester Central in 1884. The opening of the Midland direct line through Disley tunnel in 1902 ended its use of the Romiley link for most expresses, but this line kept services to Sheffield, Derby and occasionally St Pancras until closure in 1967. Most of the link's course can be seen alongside the current Bredbury–Romiley line, also opened in 1875 as a MS&L/Midland Joint link from Ashburys on the line into Manchester from Guide Bridge. Built with this link was one from Reddish Junction to

Brinnington Junction on the Stockport–Woodley line, giving a third option for trains heading east from Tiviot Dale. These were initially CLC services to London Road (from Liverpool Brunswick) but they ended with the opening of Central station in 1880. By 1903 its chief use was for fifteen GCR weekday trains (three on Sundays) from Tiviot Dale to London Road, but such services ended by 1918. The line stayed in use for freight until 1965, but was then lifted and the trackbed is now a footpath leading to the one through Brinnington tunnel.

# Woodley to Godley

Godley Junction for Liverpool? This seems an unlikely claim for station nameboards at a remote country station over 43 miles from Liverpool by rail, yet this was the case early in the 20th century. In 1903 passengers could alight at this spot from a

*Class B1 4-6-0 no 1225 is still in LNER livery in this May 1948 photo, taken at Godley before electrification. (J.A. Peden collection)*

145

*The remains of the former Godley Junction station, later Godley East. It closed in 1986 in favour of a station nearer the village (although the CLC portion had closed much earlier). (Author)*

GCR Marylebone–Manchester express and catch one of three weekday connecting trains for Liverpool (with one on Sundays). Godley Junction was the easternmost point on the CLC network, at the end of a 2 mile link from Apethorne Junction, where it was separated from the rest of the system by ⅓ mile of MS&L/Midland Joint tracks through Woodley station, which is still in use. It was built by the MS&L and opened in 1866, when Godley station on the Woodhead line was given separate CLC platforms, which stayed in use until 1962.

Far more important was freight, as this was a key link of the Liverpool–Woodhead–Sheffield and Hull route. Extensive sidings were provided, and these became vital after 1954, when the electrification of the Woodhead line meant that Godley became the changeover point between electric and steam traction for Liverpool-bound goods trains. At Brookfold on the ex-CLC line close to the junction, a turntable and facilities for coal and water were provided for the steam locomotives. These facilities became disused with the end of steam in 1968, but the line continued in use for freight until the closure of Woodhead in 1980. The route was still intact in 2000 when Sustrans bought most of it for conversion to a path for walkers and cyclists. This does not quite reach Godley, but the route is still walkable past the abandoned turntable pit to the former junction station, not used since 1986.

# Conclusion

Two scenes linger from the research for this book. The first is the former Whelley Loop's Douglas Viaduct north of Wigan. It is a mere ¼ mile from the West Coast Main Line, yet can only be reached by a narrow potholed track, followed by a scramble down the valleyside. Its 1,000 ft length of crumbling brick and rusting ironwork lies hidden in the encroaching vegetation, almost resembling some vast structure from a vanished civilisation, awaiting discovery by intrepid explorers!

The second scene is almost thirty miles away at the eastern limit of this book's coverage – the former Godley Junction station. While not so hidden away, at first glance this shows similar characteristics. There are abandoned platforms, collapsing shelters and a fenced-off footbridge, while research reveals that a once-separate set of platforms has disappeared completely. So we have a similar image of decline and decay, except for one crucial difference – there is still a working railway. Yes, trains no longer stop here, and the Great Central expresses to Marylebone and electric-hauled freight trains through Woodhead tunnel have long gone, but a ½ hourly passenger service, even on Sundays, passes through to link Manchester Piccadilly with Glossop and Hadfield. Even goods traffic may yet return if the proposed Central Railway scheme goes ahead.

These two examples set the pattern for closures within the area. Around 60% of the mileage of track used for passenger trains has survived, but under 45% of the stations are still in use. An examination of the 150 or so miles of line closures shows that this was a lengthy process. It began in 1917, only 11 years after the last opening, with the loss of local services on the Micklehurst Loop. There were few closures before 1945, but from then until 1963 and the Beeching measures, 25 lines were shut to passenger traffic, well over half those listed in the

148

summary table. Thus this was not an area whose railways were mainly 'axed' in the Beeching Report, although the inhabitants of Leigh and Tyldesley would disagree. So might people in Crosby and Radcliffe, but for the development of Merseyrail and Metrolink respectively. While only the former might be regarded as a 'true' railway, the latter has kept lines such as that to Bury open and may yet revive services to Withington and Didsbury, closed in the 1960s.

In general the two cities of Liverpool and Manchester have survived the rundown of rail services in the late 20th century reasonably well. Both have lost terminal stations and some suburban lines, although the latter were largely little-used circuitous routes, but most long-distance routes have survived, along with many suburban services thanks to Merseyrail and the Metrolink scheme. Apart from station closures within the cities, it is the 'outer' areas of the region that have lost most services. These include the area's few rural locations such as Parkgate and Delph, additional lines to places such as St Helens and Wigan, and secondary links between towns such as Bolton and Bury, and Oldham and Stockport. Although the cities have the best known railway heritage sites, such as Liverpool Road station, it is at the very edges of the area that much of interest can be seen, both at remote sites such as the Douglas Viaduct and Godley, and more accessible locations such as Hadlow Road station and the East Lancashire Railway. This is certainly an area with much to offer in terms of 'lost railways'.

# Opening and Final Closure Dates of Lines and Principal Stations to Regular Passenger Traffic

| Line | Opened | Final Closure |
|---|---|---|
| Liverpool Road Station (Manchester) | 17.9.1830 | 6.5.1844 |
| Bolton Great Moor Street/Pennington Junction | 13.6.1831 | 29.3.1954 |
| Pennington Junction/Kenyon Junction | 13.6.1831 | 5.5.1969 |
| The St Helens Railway | 21.2.1833 | 18.6.1951 |
| Castleton/Heywood | 15.4.1841 | 5.10.1970 |
| Middleton Junction/Oldham Werneth | 31.3.1842 | 2.6.1958 |
| Clifton Junction/Bury Bolton Street | 28.9.1846 | 5.12.1966 |
| Oldham Werneth/Oldham Mumps | 1.11.1847 | after May 2004 |
| Heywood/Bury Knowsley Street | 1.5.1848 | 5.10.1970[1] |
| Bury Knowsley Street/Bolton Trinity Street | 20.11.1848 | 5.10.1970 |
| Exchange Station (Liverpool) | 13.5.1850 | 2.5.1977 |
| Greenfield/Delph | 1.9.1851 | 2.5.1955 |
| Greenfield/Oldham Mumps (LNWR) | 5.7.1856 | 2.5.1955 |
| Middleton Junction/Middleton | 1.5.1857 | 7.9.1964 |
| Oldham/Ashton/Guide Bridge | 26.8.1861 | 4.5.1959 |
| Woodley/Stockport Portwood | 12.1.1863 | 6.3.1967 |
| Royton Junction/Royton | 21.3.1864 | 18.4.1966 |
| Tyldesley/Wigan | 1.9.1864 | 2.11.1964 |

[1]Reopened as an extension to the East Lancashire Railway on 7.9.2003

| Line | Opened | Final Closure |
|---|---|---|
| Eccles/Tyldesley/Leigh/Pennington Junction | 1.9.1864 | 5.5.1969 |
| Skelton Junction/Stockport Tiviot Dale | 1.12.1865 | 30.11.1964[2] |
| Apethorne Junction/Godley Junction | 1.2.1866 | 5.3.1962 |
| Hooton/Parkgate | 1.10.1866 | 17.9.1956 |
| Edge Hill/Canada Dock | 1.7.1870 | 5.5.1941[3] |
| Glazebrook/Skelton Junction | 1.3.1873 | 30.11.1964 |
| Central Station (Liverpool) | 1.3.1874 | 17.4.1972 |
| Roe Green Junction/Bolton Great Moor Street | 1.4.1875 | 29.3.1954 |
| Bredbury Junction/Romiley | 1.4.1875 | 2.1.1967 |
| Reddish Junction/Brinnington Junction | 2.8.1875 | by 1918 |
| Denton Junction/Crowthorn Junction | 1.4.1876 | by 1951 |
| Birkenhead Woodside | 31.3.1878 | 6.11.1967 |
| Halewood/Aintree (CLC) | 1.12.1879 | 7.11.1960[4] |
| Bradley Fold/Radcliffe | 1.12.1879 | 21.9.1953 |
| Throstle Nest East Junction/Heaton Mersey Junction | 1.1.1880 | 2.1.1967 |
| Central Station (Manchester) | 1.7.1880 | 5.5.1969 |
| Alexandra Dock branch | 1.9.1881 | 31.5.1948[5] |
| Ashton Moss Junction/Droylsden | 1.3.1882 | Sept 1962[6] |
| Glazebrook/Wigan | 1.4.1884 | 2.11.1964 |
| Exchange Station (Manchester) | 30.6.1884 | 5.5.1969 |
| Parkgate/West Kirby | 19.4.1886 | 17.9.1956 |
| The Micklehurst Loop | 3.5.1886 | 1.1.1917 |
| The Fallowfield Loop | 2.5.1892[7] | 7.7.1958 |
| Liverpool Overhead Railway | 6.3.1893 | 31.12.1956 |
| Denton Junction/Stalybridge | 7.8.1893 | 25.9.1950 |
| Bidston/Seacombe & Egremont | 1.6.1895 | 4.1.1960 |

[2]Skelton Junction to Northenden Junction returned to passenger service in 1988
[3]Canada Dock only; remaining stations closed with Alexandra Dock
[4]Halewood to Gateacre up to 17.4.1972
[5]In use for trains to Southport until 1977
[6]Services to Colne ended 8.9.1962
[7]Opened to Fallowfield 1.9.1891

151

| Line | Opened | Final Closure |
|---|---|---|
| Edge Hill/Riverside | 12.6.1895 | 1.3.1971 |
| Lowton St Mary's/St Helens Central | 3.1.1900 | 3.3.1952 |
| Heaton Mersey Junction/Cheadle Heath | 1.10.1901 | 2.1.1967 |
| Pennington/Platt Bridge | 1.10.1903 | 4.5.1942 |
| North Mersey branch | 1.6.1906 | 2.4.1951 |

Not included: Whelley Loop 1.1.1872 to 1.3.1872, Walton-on-the-Hill 1.12.1879 to 1.1.1918, Huskisson 2.8.1880 to 30.4.1885

Note: Closure dates are those posted by the operating company, usually a Monday, with the last train on the previous Saturday/Sunday. The dates are mostly for the withdrawal of regular stopping services using that line. Many lines continued to have through services and/or specials after the date given.

# Bibliography

Some of the following are out of print, but can still be obtained second-hand or consulted in libraries.

Bolger, P. *Merseyside and District Railway Stations* (Bluecoat Press)

Bolger, P. *The Docker's Umbrella* (Bluecoat Press)

Fox, G.T. *Stockport Tiviot Dale* (Foxline Publishing)

Fox, M. & P. *The Delph Donkey* (M. & P. Fox)

Gahan, J.W. *Seventeen Stations to Dingle* (Countyvise/ AvonAnglia)

Gahan, J.W. *Steel Wheels to Deeside* (Countyvise/AvonAnglia)

Goode, C.T. *The Railways of Manchester* (C.T. Goode)

Griffiths, R.P. *The Cheshire Lines Railway* (The Oakwood Press)

Holland, Bert *Plodder Lane for Farnworth* (Triangle Publishing)

Holt, G.O. *A Regional History of the Railways of Great Britain: Volume 10: The North West* (David & Charles)

Hooper, J. *An Illustrated History of Oldham's Railways* (Irwell Press)

Johnson, E.M. *Railways in and around the Manchester Suburbs* (Foxline Publishing)

Johnson, E.M. *The Fallowfield Line* (Foxline Publishing)

Marshall, J. *Forgotten Railways: North West England* (David & Charles)

Maund, T.B. *The Birkenhead Railway* (RCTS)

Pixton, Bob *Main Line Railways Around Wigan* (Runpast Publishing)

Pixton, Bob *Widnes and St Helens Railways* (Chalfont Publishing)

Sweeney, D.J. *A Lancashire Triangle: Volumes 1 & 2* (Triangle Publishing)

Tolson, J.M. *The St Helens Railway* (The Oakwood Press)

Townley, C.H.A., Smith, F.D. & Peden, J.A. *Industrial Railways of the Wigan Coalfield: Volume 1: West and South of Wigan* (Runpast Publishing)*

Wells, J. *Miles Platting to Diggle via Ashton* (Challenger Publications)


*This was the first in a series of six volumes on the coalfields' industrial railways. Note that later volumes have been published by the Industrial Railway Society.

# INDEX